Even Better!

Even Better!
A Guide to Winning in Life

Bill Ballester

EVEN BETTER!
A GUIDE TO WINNING IN LIFE

iUniverse books may be ordered through booksellers or by contacting:

iUniverse
1663 Liberty Drive
Bloomington, IN 47403
www.iuniverse.com
1-800-Authors (1-800-288-4677)

Because of the dynamic nature of the Internet, any web addresses or links contained in this book may have changed since publication and may no longer be valid. The views expressed in this work are solely those of the author and do not necessarily reflect the views of the publisher, and the publisher hereby disclaims any responsibility for them.

Any people depicted in stock imagery provided by Thinkstock are models, and such images are being used for illustrative purposes only.

Certain stock imagery © Thinkstock.

ISBN: 978-1-4759-7294-8 (sc)
ISBN: 978-1-4759-7295-5 (hc)
ISBN: 978-1-4759-7296-2 (e)

Library of Congress Control Number: 2013901359

Print information available on the last page.

iUniverse rev. date: 05/17/2019

To my father, Earl Ballester, who provided the kick-start (literally, the kick in the pants) that got me through the first years of my life. His determination to impart life's values, the meaning of self-discipline, and the need for hard work has been my constant companion throughout life.

To Bill Meade, my coach, my mentor, and my friend, who provided me with the opportunity, the encouragement, and the confidence to achieve my dreams. Thanks, Coach!

And to my mom, Gladys Ballester, for providing unconditional love and support. Her words of encouragement have provided the strength and confidence for me to address life's challenges head-on. We look forward to celebrating her 104th birthday in 2013!

Contents

Preface   ix
Acknowledgments   xix
Part One: The Journey to Winning in Life   1

Chapter 1 Can I Be Your Coach?   3

    Are You Coachable?   4
    Listening   5

Chapter 2 Are We Speaking the Same Language?   9

    Effective Communication   9

Chapter 3 Change   17

    Change in Leadership Style   18
    Change in Business and Government   20
    Change in Thinking: Scarcity to Abundance   22
    Scarcity/Abundance Thinking in Families   26

Chapter 4 Two Different Teams, Two Different Results   31

    The Dream   33
    Agreements   36

Part Two: A Leadership Model for Winning Teams   47
Part Three: The Nine Principles of Winning Teams   53

    Principle #1: The Double Win   53
    Principle #2: Adaptation   55
    Principle #3: Alignment   58
    Principle #4: Contribution   62
    Principle #5: Responsible Freedom   73
    Principle #6: Integrity   80
    Principle #7: Positive Learning Cycle   82
    Principle #8: The Balance of Extremes   89
    Principle #9: Progressive Mastery   96

Part Four: How to Solve Problems   101

Chapter 5 Is There a Secret to Winning?   103

    Communication: No Good News/No Bad News   105

Chapter 6 Adventure in Baja   109

    Understanding Destructive Conflict   115
    Formula for Resolving Destructive Conflict   119

Chapter 7 Now Who Do We Blame?   121

    Focus   125
    Team Checklist   128
    When to Solve a Problem   137
    Our Race in Baja   138
    ABCDE Problem-Solving Formula   141
    Why, Why, Why, Why, Why?   148

Part Five: Tools for Life   **151**

    Our Journey Together   152
    Invitation   153

Appendix A   **155**
Appendix B   **157**

Preface
Why Read This Book?

Our entire lives are spent looking for answers, answers that we hope will guide us to become Even Better at everything we do; however, before we can find those answers, we must first find the right questions.

Are you willing to accept the possibility that you can become Even Better?

1. Even Better as a partner in your personal relationships?
2. Even Better as a parent?
3. Even Better as a grandparent?
4. Even Better as a business or government leader?
5. Even Better as a coach?
6. Even Better in all aspects of your life?

If your answer to any of these questions is *yes,* congratulations! By acknowledging that you would like to become Even Better at something, anything, you have also acknowledged that there is room for improvement, that you are not perfect. This is a great (and essential) first step. Read on!

Have you ever asked yourself *why* some people or some teams consistently win while others fail?

- Why do some coaches always seem to win, regardless of where they go to coach?
- Why do some business leaders always create highly motivated and productive employees?
- Why do some parents provide the leadership that creates successful children?
- Why do some government leaders get so much done while many others seem to falter?

Here are some other questions:

- Are great leaders born?
- Does leadership require some special type of personality?
- Can anyone become a great leader?
- Can leaders who have failed overcome their problems and achieve success?
- Is there a common thread, a common set of principles or tools, that all great leaders possess?

Even Better! will give you the answers to these and many more questions. *Even Better!* will guide, direct, and support you on your personal journey through life and provide the necessary tools for you to become Even Better in all of your relationships.

I encourage you to read with an open mind and at the same time read with the intention of finding answers to all of your questions about teams and team leadership.

What do we really know about teams?

Many of us only associate teams with sports, but there are many other types of teams.

There are business teams, government teams, and family teams. Some teams are small, and some are very large; there are some teams that win, while there are some teams that lose; there are some teams that are very effective, and there are other teams that are ineffective.

We are all on teams, some by birth, some by accident, some by choice. We enjoy some of our teams; we dislike others—but regardless how we feel about teams, we all participate on many teams!

Human history is the story of teams and teamwork. From the

beginning of time, individuals have learned that to survive (and ultimately prosper), they had to work together. Out of necessity teams were formed, families were created, communities were developed, religions were founded, governments were created, wars were fought, businesses were launched, and unions were organized—all for the purpose of doing things more effectively. For the world, for our governments, for our businesses, and for our families to survive and prosper, we must learn and apply the basic concepts of teamwork and team building.

Even Better! is a breakthrough in thinking about teams and our relationships with others, about how we can successfully live our lives in peace and with happiness.

Who in the Heck Is Bill Ballester?

Before you read any more or ask any more questions about "Why" and "How," I would like to share with you a little more about me, Bill Ballester—the person, the coach, and the parent—and what led me to write this book. My personal journey toward my dreams has not always been smooth; It has been a lifelong search to identify those dreams and then learn how to make them a reality.

I learned early in life that I needed money to do the things that I enjoyed. I also learned from my father that if I wanted money and the things that money could bring me, I would have to go out and earn it for myself. My first lesson came when I was about nine years old. I asked Dad if I could have a bicycle; he said, "Sure, how are you going to pay for it?"

After a few tears and a lot of thinking about that bicycle, I answered, "I will go to work." That answer led me to my first real job: delivering newspapers. (Having to get up at five in the morning to deliver newspapers was not something that I enjoyed.)

A few years later, I got a new job as a dishwasher in a small restaurant and soon moved on to become a busboy. (I wasn't real excited about those jobs either.) I continued to work at various jobs through my high school years. Once out of high school, I went to work in the industrial labor force, working at various factory jobs near Chicago. (I didn't like most of these jobs either, but they provided the money for me to buy the things that I wanted.)

During those early years of working at jobs that I really didn't like, I also learned about things that I did like. I liked adventure, excitement, fast cars, and bouncing on trampolines.

As a young adult, I had no plans for my future, no dreams beyond the next day, aside from making enough money to have fun and to keep my old car running. I had no long-term goals. I only knew that I was very unhappy with the work that I was doing. It was during one of those long days working on an assembly line in a factory that I began to think that maybe college should become my next adventure, my next chance to have fun. With a few dollars that I had managed to save, I enrolled at Southern Illinois University. I had no particular interest in any area of study, only a desire to maximize enjoyment in my life.

I managed to make it through my first year at Southern while having fun, enjoying the new adventure, and not flunking out of school. After a year of college, I still didn't have any long-term dreams or goals, but one afternoon early in my second year, while walking across campus, I passed the gym and spotted a trampoline. Never one to pass up an opportunity to do something exciting, I quickly took off my shoes, climbed onto the trampoline, and started to bounce.

Although I was not blessed with much skill or experience, I did know how to have fun. I was so busy having fun that nearly an hour passed, and I didn't even notice that I was no longer alone in the gym. A man came over and introduced himself as Bill Meade, Southern's new men's gymnastics coach. Coach Meade and I visited for a while, and he invited me to try out for his team. That invitation changed my life.

Coach Meade had a huge impact on my life, as my coach, as my mentor, and later as my good friend. I had finally found something that I really enjoyed and discovered a coach and a team that welcomed me as a team member.

I spent the next few years bouncing my way through college as a gymnast and finally discovered what I really wanted to do with my life. That singular event—going into the gym that day and meeting Bill Meade—was the beginning of my dream to become a gymnastics coach. While I told myself that I wanted to become one of the best gymnastics coaches in the country, it wouldn't be a stretch to say that

I *really* wanted to become one of the best gymnastics coaches in the world. I had finally found my dream: a really big one!

Looking back now at that dream, it seems completely unrealistic. Fortunately, I did not know how unlikely it was that my dream would ever become a reality. Keep in mind that I had never been involved in any organized sport; I had never been a part of any athletic team. I should also disclose that I never became an outstanding gymnast. In fact, I wasn't even a very good gymnast. However, I did have a great coach. And I had a big dream. Despite my lack of skill and experience, Coach Meade always encouraged me to work toward my dream of someday becoming a gymnastics coach. (Coach Bill Meade's teams won four NCAA championships; he went on to coach many Olympians and was inducted into every possible Hall of Fame for gymnastics. Yes! Bill Meade was a great coach, a great husband and father, and a great inspiration for me.)

Graduating from SIU was the first step to attaining my dream. My coaching career started when I was hired as an assistant men's gymnastics coach, assistant football coach, and assistant tennis coach at East Leyden High School in Franklin Park, Illinois, a suburb of Chicago. The following year, I became the head gymnastics coach at Waukegan Township High School, where I spent the next ten years teaching physical education and coaching men's gymnastics, track, and swimming.

The next step toward realizing my dream was at the University of Wisconsin, Parkside, teaching and coaching men's gymnastics. It was there that I had the opportunity to work for Dr. Thomas Rosandich, who became another important mentor in my life. My years as a high school coach and my one year at Parkside gave me the chance to work with many great young men.

After eleven years, I moved one step closer to realizing my dreams when I was hired to coach men's gymnastics at the University of Oregon. While I was moving closer to my dream, Dr. Rosandich was also pursuing his dream: to establish a university dedicated to the training of sports professionals. In 1972, he established the United States Sports Academy, located in Daphne, Alabama, which is now the largest graduate school of sports education in the world.

For more than twenty-five years I had the opportunity to live my dream, coaching men's gymnastics at many different levels. With each level came more challenges, more opportunities, and more movement toward my dream of being the best gymnastics coach in America. Those years seemed to fly by; looking back now, I realize that the most significant reward from my coaching career was not watching my teams succeed, it was watching student athletes grow and develop, not only as outstanding gymnasts, but as fine young men.

In 1981, my dream was shattered. In spite of our successful record, winning many conference championships, and strong student and community support, the University of Oregon dropped men's gymnastics. The gymnastics team had been considered one of the premier programs in the country, and all of a sudden, it was no more. It was devastating for me to see the program shut down; at the time, there was little comfort in knowing that we had accomplished many of our individual and team goals and were always a credit to the university and the community. I was bitter, confused, and angry.

I spent the next five years upside down, without a dream and without goals; all that was left of my dream was frustration and resentment. I still worked at the university, with various responsibilities that included NCAA compliance officer, student conduct coordinator, and liaison between the local police and fraternities/sororities.

However, I wasn't coaching gymnastics, and I didn't have the same love for my new work. I quickly learned that my passion for coaching had been my reason to get up each day, to go to work, to live. It was only when my dream was gone that I truly became aware of how important it was (and is!) for me to have a dream and to be able to spend my life pursuing it.

A New Dream

One day, while having a cup of coffee with my friend Larry Spencer, a new dream began to emerge. As avid sports followers, we began to talk about an observation that we had each made over a period of many years: some coaches always seemed to win, regardless of where they were coaching and regardless of the circumstances. Conversely, others seemed almost destined to lose. The more we thought about it, the more examples we found that supported our theory.

We also speculated that there might be similarities among highly successful coaches whose teams continue to win over long periods of time. We wondered if they all might be doing some of the same things. Were there common values, common techniques, common methods, or common leadership styles among all winning coaches? Were there similar principles that all winning coaches used? Moreover, if our beliefs were correct and if we could discover those similarities, could the same leadership strategies be applied to the world of business and government? Could we develop a leadership model from sports that could be used by leaders in a variety of teams? Excited about this possibility, Larry and I decided to create a series of questions that we could use to interview highly successful coaches.

Over the next few years, we met with more than seventy of the top coaches in the country, representing eleven different sports. The group included coaches of young children, coaches of high school and college athletes, and coaches of professional athletes. We interviewed both male and female coaches, representing a variety of different coaching styles from many different parts of the country.

We spent the next two years sorting through all of our notes, looking for the similarities, and after many hours of discussions (and quite a few arguments), we finally agreed that there were nine basic principles that all of the coaches utilized. We call them the "Nine Principles of Winning Teams." These principles will be discussed in detail in Part 2.

I began to speak at Rotary clubs and other leadership functions to share our research. After that, I began to interview leaders from business and government to learn if they used similar principles. During one interview, a very successful businesswoman asked me if those same principles from the world of sports could be used to help families. Could these same Nine Principles of Winning Teams be used in our families, with our children, with our parents, with our spouses or partners? Her question made me expand my original thinking. I realized that the Nine Principles of Winning Teams could be used to successfully develop teams in all human relationships.

As the research and development process continued to unfold, I began to realize that I could once again coach: I could coach other coaches and athletes from all sports; I could coach business and government leaders and their team members; I could even coach parents and their children. I could once again pursue my dream of coaching. With that realization, I left the university, excited to begin my new adventure and pursue my new dream. I was once again living my life with passion.

For the next fifteen years, I was able to share my thoughts about winning, teamwork, and the Nine Principles of Winning Teams with thousands of people, at national and regional conferences, private companies, and government agencies from coast to coast. I worked with teams of all sizes, from couples in a relationship to the US Department of Transportation (I worked as their national spokesman for team building and teamwork). I worked with doctors, dentists, and their support teams. I worked with large construction companies, their leaders, and their team members. During those fifteen years, I continued to gather more and more tools to effectively implement the principles into all teams. Yes, I was once again coaching, sharing my thoughts and ideas about winning and teamwork with a much larger team: the human team.

Now I am pursuing my newest coaching dream: sharing my thoughts, ideas, and the Nine Principles of Winning Teams with even more people, by writing this book.

Writing *Even Better!* may be my greatest coaching challenge ever, once again starting fresh with little more than my dream, with no knowledge or experience of what it takes to write a book. I started with many unanswered questions, starting with: should I write a series of books, each about a specific team? A book designed for sports, a book designed for business, a book designed for government, and a book designed for parenting? My answer was no. Our lives are not separated in orderly boxes; our teams are all interrelated, and the same Nine Principles of Winning Teams apply to all of them.

My most difficult question to answer: how do I express my ideas in writing? One of my strengths as a coach is my ability to communicate verbally. I am able to convey my thoughts with confidence, excitement, and enthusiasm. How can I do that in a book?

After many attempts to put my thoughts to paper, I realized that writing was not one of my strengths. I finally decided to write like I speak, write as if I were talking with you, by telling stories about coaching, stories about racing, stories about raising children, stories about my personal struggles and victories, stories that come from my heart. I have always been more concerned with the results of my coaching than with how I looked or how I sounded or if my presentations were up to industry standards. *Even Better!* was not written to be acknowledged as a literary accomplishment, it was written for you, to share my thoughts and ideas with you in a way that can change your life.

As you are reading *Even Better!* you may, at times, find yourself saying, "I know that" or "This is repetitive."

I realize that many of these ideas are not new to you; however, I don't know which ideas will change your life and which ones you already understand and already effectively apply. I have also intentionally repeated and stressed key concepts in order to make essential points.

Even Better! is an unconventional, nontraditional book that has many thoughts and ideas that are considered out of the ordinary. If you continue reading this book, you have decided to move beyond ordinary, to become Even Better, to become extraordinary!

Acknowledgments

Soon after reaching one of my primary goals—graduating from college—I found myself reaching simultaneously for my two most important dreams: being a good parent and becoming a successful gymnastics coach. During those first few years, it seemed that there were never enough hours in a day, or days in the week, to do either job well. As I look back now, it is very evident that my children, Robin Kennett, Kelli Gilliam, and Bill Ballester, along with their mother, Marilyn Ballester, were not only tolerant of my coaching commitments, they were incredibly supportive. I now fully appreciate that my journey has been blessed with the love and support of my family.

I also want to thank all of the young men who gave me the opportunity to coach them; together we learned many of life's values, celebrated life's rewards, and experienced a few of life's setbacks. With the assistance of Larry Spencer and the many coaches, business leaders, and parents whom we interviewed, we developed the model for winning in all of our teams: the Nine Principles of Winning Teams.

As I continue my journey, I know that those many wonderful, yet demanding, years provided for me the foundation, the tools, the desire, and the motivation to complete this book. The desire to complete *Even Better!* is a direct result of what each member of my family—and my extended family of team members, supporters, and advocates—have contributed to make my dreams a reality.

Finally, I'd like to thank everyone who contributed to the logistics of preparing and publishing this book, from the early stages of development, involving Camille Courtright, Jack Peters, Bradley Bjornstad, and Ellen Nichols—who provided ideas and direction—to the final steps, involving Lindsay Ramirez, and the editing staff at iUniverse, who provided the professional support and candid feedback to complete the manuscript.

Part One:

The Journey to Winning in Life

Life is a journey, a continuous learning experience, fueled by the constant search to become Even Better! I invite you to join me to take this journey to winning together. Before you consider my invitation, I have a few questions for you to answer for yourself:

Do you like to win?

Do you want to be happy?

Do you want to be healthy?

Do you want to be respected?

Do you want to feel of value to yourself and others?

Do you want to be trusted?

Do you want to trust others?

Do you want to have a prosperous life?

Do you believe that you can improve, to get Even Better?

Do you want to improve, to get Even Better?

I have asked these and similar questions to every group of people I have worked with during the last fifteen years, from groups as diverse as visiting Russian Rotarians and sports administrators in Hong Kong to American business and government leaders and their hourly workers. I have asked these same questions to parents, grandparents, and children.

And you know what? Everyone has responded with exactly the same answer: YES, for every question.

Did you answer these questions with "Yes"? If that is the case, then we have taken the first step necessary for our journey by recognizing and acknowledging similarities among all people, including you and me. I call these similarities "samenesses."

We have established that you want to win and that you want to learn more about how to win. Are you ready for our journey together? Great!

Before we start, I am going to ask you one more simple but very important question: Can I be your coach?

Chapter 1
Can I Be Your Coach?

Take a few more minutes to look inside yourself and react to this question before you answer it. Your degree of acceptance will significantly affect our journey together. Before answering, I will tell you what the word "coach" means to me: a coach is a leader who is committed to serving the team and the individuals on the team. A coach has the responsibility to create an environment that will allow each team member to grow and develop to his or her greatest level of potential. In other words, a coach exists only to provide an environment for all team members to meet their personal goals while helping the team reach its goals and objectives.

If you agree to let me be your coach, expect to learn how to win on all of your teams, expect to become an Even Better parent or grandparent, expect to become an Even Better leader with all of your teams. Don't worry, there won't be any push-ups or running laps. So what about it? Can I be your coach? I am asking you to make a commitment to me as your coach and to your own life, a commitment to learn how you can become Even Better in all of your relationships. Once a commitment is made, the process of change will begin.

About Commitment

> Until one is committed, there is hesitancy, the chance to draw back, always ineffectiveness. Concerning all acts of initiative (and creation) there is one elementary truth, the ignorance of which kills countless ideas and splendid plans: that the moment one definitely commits oneself, then Providence moves too. A whole stream of events issues from the decision, raising in one's favor all manner of unforeseen incidents, meetings and material assistance, which no man could have dreamt would have come his way. I learned a deep respect for one of Goethe's couplets:
>
> > *Whatever you can do or dream you can, begin it.*
> > *Boldness has genius, power and magic in it!*
>
> —*W. H. Murray*

If you are still with me, then you have made a commitment to yourself and to me as your coach to explore your opportunities for additional growth and development, to create an Even Better life for yourself and those you come in contact with. We have established that you like to win and that you have agreed to be coached by me. Fantastic!

My next question is, are you coachable?

Are You Coachable?

What does being coachable mean to you? As you think about your answer, let's explore together what being coachable means to me. When I think of being coachable, I think of the following characteristics: enthusiasm, excitement, commitment, the willingness to change, the willingness to listen, the desire to learn and grow, and finally the unyielding desire to improve, to become Even Better at everything you do.

Are you coachable? A good place for you to find this answer is to become aware of how you are receiving this information. How are you listening? Are you open to learn? Are you critical? Cynical? Accepting? Bored? Excited? Your answers to these questions will help you to determine if you are really coachable.

I will be asking you many questions throughout our journey together. When I have a question for you, or you have a question about what you are reading, stop reading and take a few minutes to reflect and answer these questions for yourself. I encourage you to read this book and to live your life constantly asking "Why" and "How" questions.

Listening

Being willing to listen is an essential part of being coachable. (Even though you are reading, your response to what you read is a form of listening.)

Listening can mean many different things. Growing up, I was taught to listen to what I was told, to keep my mouth shut, and to look into the eyes of the person who was talking. Even though I did these things, there were many occasions that I learned very little because I was not listening with an open mind.

Become aware of how you listen; are you open to consider that what you are reading (listening to) is possible? Are you willing to consider the possibility that what you read might work for you and maybe even change your life? At the very least, ask yourself, "What if I can become an Even Better leader or parent?"

If you are closed to an idea, and you have already made a decision, there is no real listening. Without listening, there is no learning, and without considering the possibility that you may learn something by listening, you are not coachable. What's going on in your mind right now? Are you still coachable? Are you still open to possibility? Are you willing to consider that *Even Better!* can actually change your life?

We all can become Even Better listeners when we make a conscious effort to become aware of how we really listen. We can discover if we are closing our mind to what we are hearing because we don't like a person's age, race, nationality, sex, or even political views.

All humans have what I call "built-in" listening. We will listen to someone based on what we feel we will gain from listening. What would happen if I told you that in this book, I will tell you how to become an instant millionaire? How would you listen to me then? Would you casually glance through the next few pages at your leisure, or would you commit every ounce of your energy to discover what I would share with you? How we listen is tied directly to what we feel we will gain from listening. This isn't good and it isn't bad—it is simply part of being human. My coaching suggestion: listen to everything as if you will learn something that will change your life, and be open to learn from everyone.

I want to share one other observation about listening: the closer you are to someone—such as your spouse, your children, your parents, your boss, or your employees—the less "listening" is actually happening, by anyone. Remember, there is no listening when you have already made up your mind.

Nearly every leader has a so-called "open door policy." They may say things like, "Come on in, my door is always open," or "What's on your mind?" or "Of course I value your input." You may have heard similar statements from your own parents. But sometimes, even after we are assured that there will be open listening, it does not happen.

It may be useful to share a personal story that illustrates my own lack of listening. When my daughters were very young, I told them that I was willing to listen to them about anything they wanted to talk about. I also told them that my decisions were made with consideration of their input. When they were about fifteen or sixteen years old, they came to me with a request that lingers in my mind, even after all of these years. They asked, "Dad, can we stay out until four o'clock next Friday night?"

After a few deep breaths and an internal conversation (that I won't share here), I started to ask rather pointed questions like, "Why do you want to stay out until four o'clock Friday night? Where do you want to go? Who do you want to go with?"

Even while acknowledging their answers, there was absolutely no "listening" by me! Why? Because I had made up my mind long before our conversation ended that there was no way I was going to permit them to stay out until four that night, regardless of what they said to me.

Can you relate to this scenario in any way? Have you found yourself "tuning out" in a conversation, or being tuned out? What are you missing by not listening? What are they missing by not really listening to you? What might be learned that would be of value to you or to the other person if everyone was really listening with a mind that was open to possibilities?

Coaching Hint

Constantly be aware of how you are listening to those around you.

Also, be aware of the possibility that others may not really be listening to you. Everyone is human and subject to the same problems with their listening. Often in businesses, families, and even sports teams, there is little or no listening going on by anyone. Coaches often don't really listen to their players, players don't really listen to their coaches, bosses really don't listen to their employees, and employees really don't listen to their bosses. Parents and children really don't listen to each other either. *Why* is there so little real listening? Good question. Because many have closed their minds to the possibility that there might be something of value for them if they really listened. What can not listening cost you with your loved ones and your fellow team members? Without open listening, there is no effective communication, and effective communication is an essential part of team building and winning in life.

How is your listening right now? Are you still listening with an open mind? Great!

Chapter 2
Are We Speaking the Same Language?

Effective Communication

"What did you say?" "Say it again, please." "I don't understand." "One more time, please." I can't count the number of times that I have heard or spoken those words. I spent many years visiting Baja, Mexico, and I enjoy the culture and the people; however, I do not speak their language. I have tried to learn Spanish, and I can communicate (a little), but there are times when I just can't seem to understand the person I am talking with. I frequently use a dictionary or translator to make sure I am using the correct words; however, even with direct translation from English to Spanish, words can mean different things to different people. My experiences in Mexico have helped me to become more aware that my words don't always convey my meaning and that my words may not mean the same thing to others. This chapter is written to minimize any misunderstandings that may occur between us caused by our different use of certain thoughts and words. Our journey together will be much more effective if we have a common understanding of the meaning for words and phrases that I frequently use. Spend a little time reading through these definitions and phrases and their meaning to me.

Bill Ballester

What Is a Team?

There are lots of different definitions for *team*. However, as your coach, I would encourage you to adopt my simple and straightforward understanding of this term:

A team is two or more people who come together to accomplish something that they could not otherwise accomplish as well alone.

Using this definition, you can see that we all are on many teams. Sometimes being a member of a team occurs by circumstance or default. We don't choose to be a member of the human team, and yet, by our existence, we are. There are many teams that we become members of by choice: joining the school band, a sorority or fraternity, the local Rotary club, and athletic teams are choices that we each make individually. Finally, even though we don't usually think of them as such, we are involved in many different relationships and groups that are teams. Your family is a team (parents, children, relatives), you and your spouse are a team, you and your car mechanic are a team, and you and your doctor are a team. Any time that two or more people work together to do something they can't do as well alone, there is a team.

Here are some teams of which I am a member:

- The human team
- The USA team
- My family team (my parents, children, relatives)
- My work team
- My community team
- My Rotary team
- My readers and me (that's you!)

I encourage you to consider the many teams to which you belong; think about each of your teams and ask yourself, why am I on this team, what do I gain by being a member of this team, what can I do to make my team Even Better?

What Is a Dream?

A dream is a visualization of a desired result. One of my first memories of dreaming happened in the first grade. I was just sitting there, looking out the window, and dreaming of going fishing in a small creek near my uncle's home in northern Indiana. I really wanted to go fishing; I could practically smell the water as I envisioned myself sitting on the bank with a bamboo pole in hand and a can of worms at my side. This dream became a reality later that summer, when my uncle invited me to spend a few weeks working on his farm. And it was remembering that dream that provided the inspiration for me to accept his invitation.

Unfortunately, dreaming was discouraged when I was in school. Teachers frequently told me to stop daydreaming and pay attention to what they were saying (to listen). I later found that most things big and small start from unstructured thoughts (dreams) about a desired result. Keep dreaming! It is the first step to reality.

When I refer to dreams as they pertain to teams, it means the thing that brings people together to form the team. A dream is the inspiration and visualization of a desired result; it usually starts with a single person, and that person shares his or her dream with others that have the desire to accomplish the same results, and together they form a team. Dreaming and sharing your dream are the first steps to creating a winning team.

What Is a Team Member?

Teams are composed of members: people organized under a single directive for a single purpose. In sports, there is a core group of team members: coaches and players. In families, this core group is usually the parents and the children. In business and in government, the core team is made up of employers and employees.

I will expand my definition of a team member to include anyone that impacts the team and anyone that is impacted by the team.

- In sports, this includes administrators, secretaries, equipment workers, marketing people, members of the media, family members, fans, and supporters.

- In families, grandparents, cousins, aunts and uncles, even teachers and coaches.
- In business, customers, suppliers, the communities in which we work and live, and all family members.
- In government, employees, voters, suppliers, and all those who are affected by the actions taken by the team.

This is a very expanded definition for team members, yet the list is far from being complete. This list is intended to stimulate your thinking and help you to become aware of the many people who are touched by you and each of your teams.

What Is a Team Leader?

Teams require leaders to reach their goals and objectives; leaders come in many different forms and are chosen in many different ways. Some simply surface because of their leadership qualities; others are predetermined, such as parents. Some are hired or elected, such as those in business and government. On some of our teams, we are leaders, on other teams, we are members, and in some situations we are both leaders and members.

Team leaders have many different titles. In sports, it is the coach; in families, it is usually Dad or Mom; in business, it is the president, CEO, or boss; in government, it is the president, governor, or mayor. These are just a few of the titles for team leaders. All team leaders have a primary responsibility to provide an environment in which all team members can meet their personal goals while meeting the goals and objectives of the team.

What Is Teamwork?

Teamwork is nothing more than a group of people coming together, acknowledging and recognizing their similar dreams and goals. This act, in turn, acknowledges and recognizes the need for support from one another to accomplish something that each could not accomplish as well alone. By being an active contributing member of a team, we can accomplish much more, much faster than being alone.

Why Team Building?

There are many philosophies and theories about why individuals and teams benefit from focusing on team building. I believe that a cohesive team can consistently outperform a collection of talented individuals. When team members learn to work together toward a common goal, and understand that personal goals and team objectives are interdependent, and actually help each other, they are really helping themselves.

What Is Competition?

Competition is what teams and individuals do when they want the same things: they compete for them. We usually think of competition as something that occurs in sports, where athletes and their teams compete to win championships; to determine who is the best, the strongest, the most capable; to decide who is superior.

However, all teams compete, either internally or externally. Competition occurs naturally between all living organisms that coexist in the same environment. Many philosophers and psychologists believe that competitiveness is an innate biological trait that coexists along with the urge for survival. What does this mean? Good question.

I have always thought of survival as the most basic need found in all living things, followed by the need for air, water, and food; now I am adding competitiveness to that same category. Wow! Survival, air, water, food, and competitiveness all listed as basic human needs! What do you think about competitiveness being listed as a basic human need?

I believe there are two major types of competition:

- **Healthy competition** provides incentives for improvement that lead to personal and team growth and development. My research, my coaching career, and my personal experiences have convinced me that the highest form of healthy competition is within oneself, to continually look for ways to improve upon past performances. The good news: unless you quit trying, you can't lose this personal competition. The desire to constantly improve is even more important than beating an opponent. Keep your listening open.

- **Unhealthy competition** is perhaps easier to understand; we have all seen examples of it. Symptoms of unhealthy competition are many conflicts among team members, a reluctance for team members to help each other, diminishing team productivity, high turnover among team members, cheating, dishonesty, and a lack of integrity. One type of unhealthy competition is hypercompetitiveness. Some people have a need to compete and win at any cost; winning is their way of determining and maintaining their self-worth. If they lose, they consider it failure.

The line between healthy competition and unhealthy competition can be very thin; it is a line that highly successful leaders must constantly monitor and evaluate.

What Is Winning and Success?

Winning and success are one and the same for me. I would ask you to accept that all human beings like to win. I know that winning has an infinite number of meanings unique to each person. None are more correct than others. Here is what winning means to me:

- Producing measurable results that move me and my team closer to our desired results
- Learning from my mistakes and correcting them
- Knowing that I have done everything that can be done to reach my desired results
- Never quitting

Have you noticed that winning, for me, does not involve having the best score? I call winning based on a score "Winning on Saturday." Don't for a moment think that I'm saying it isn't desired or important; I believe that it is very important, and when I talk about creating an environment for winning, I also mean Winning on Saturday. However, Winning on Saturday is a by-product of creating an environment in which everyone on the team is fully committed to improving their performance as individuals and as a team. If Winning on Saturday is your primary goal and you lose, what have you done? You have failed! You have created failure. My advice is to avoid creating a primary goal to win on Saturday, which can (and eventually will) create failure. Do you like to fail? Don't spend a lot of time right now questioning my thinking about this idea. You don't have to agree with me, just accept that it may be possible. You will become more comfortable with this thought as we continue our journey together.

What Is Losing?

Many people equate losing with having fewer points at the end of the game than the other team. Some people also say that winning and losing are opposites: if there are winners, there must be losers.

Let's take a closer look at what losing means to me. We know that nobody likes to lose. Losing can cause embarrassment and guilt; it can sometimes lead to feelings of blame and anger. So why not create your life without losing? I can almost hear you say, "How can anyone go through life without losing?" Well, a good place to start is to change your belief that winning and losing are at opposite ends of a spectrum. It's difficult, when we consistently hear the old saying from Vince Lombardi, "Winning isn't everything, it's the only thing." The great coach of the Green Bay Packers also said, "Winning is not everything, but wanting to win is," and "Winning isn't everything, but the will to win is." These last two quotes are very different in nature from the first, but unfortunately, they are not as well known. In sports, we constantly hear coaches and athletes saying, "Winning is the only thing," and this subsequently fosters the (I would argue inaccurate) belief that those who don't win are losers or failures.

I believe that losing is a frame of mind: it is your own perception of yourself and your actions. A Saturday loss in sports can create all of the negative feelings referred to above, or it can be viewed simply as a setback and an opportunity to learn, to grow, to develop and become more skilled and more capable. Ultimately, a Saturday loss can be viewed as just another step toward winning (even though at the time it sure looks and feels like losing).

What does losing mean to you? Again, losing is uniquely personal to each individual who experiences it. What are your thoughts? What does losing mean to you? Now, let go of those thoughts and find ways to change your traditional beliefs about losing. Think differently about losing; see losing as only a setback and ultimately a step closer to winning. Think of losing in a way that will create new hope, new enthusiasm, and renewed commitment.

What Is a Loser?

Losers are people who wander aimlessly through life without dreams, goals, or objectives.

This is about as close as I get to a good definition of a loser.

What Is a Problem?

When I refer to problems, I am referring to anything that stands between you and your dream, your desired results. Other words that have a similar meaning are "barriers," "roadblocks," and "obstacles."

What Are Vibrations?

"Vibration" is a word that I use to describe those things that direct attention away from the dream: anything that slows production, reduces enthusiasm, and minimizes fun. The word can be used to describe any problem found within a team. Vibrations come in many forms, from pain and sickness in our bodies to breakdowns in our cars and lack of communication among business and family team members. They are an indicator that something is in the way of the dream and in the way of success.

Chapter 3
Change

To become Even Better at anything usually requires change: change in actions, change in preparation, and many times change in thinking. Recognizing and acknowledging change, and accepting it as a given, is an important part of life and becoming Even Better.

Change can be as obvious as changing the air in our lungs with every breath we take, the changes of seasons each year, and the changes in the ocean's tide, which occur twice every day. There are also changes in how we think, changes in how we feel, and changes in how we live our lives.

Changes in the World

The Industrial Revolution is a great example of a major change; it is still creating change throughout the world.

I am not a historian, but I will share my thoughts about the major changes that led not only to changes among countries and world leaders, but changes in all of our teams. These changes were sometimes viewed as progressive, other times as conservative, sometimes as effective, and other times as destructive. Regardless, those changes had, and continue to have, an impact on how we interact with one another in government, in business, in sports, and in our families.

Change in Leadership Style

People can be divided between those who lead and those who follow. Traditionally, those who led did the thinking and decision making, while those who followed did the work to implement the leaders' decisions. Many describe this leadership model as Command and Control (C&C). The C&C model of leadership has always existed. However, it was Frederick Winslow Taylor, an American academic, who formalized this style of leadership in written texts. Based on his work, management as a science took hold in the United States in the late 1800s and continued to blossom throughout most of the twentieth century in a form often referred to as Taylorism. The basic premise in Taylor's doctrines are best described in his own words:

Hardly a competent workman can be found who does not devote considerable time to seeing just how slowly he can go and still convince his employer he is going at a good pace. Under our system a worker is told just what he is to do and how he is to do it. Any improvement he makes on the orders given him is fatal to his success.

—*Frederick Winslow Taylor,* The Principles of Scientific Management

Who was this Taylor, who so many have credited for the development of the United States into an industrial leader? I wanted to learn more. While looking for the answer, I read an article written in 1988 by Konosuke Matsushita called "Manufacturing Engineering." In that article, he proclaimed that Japanese companies would win out over US companies, saying, "You cannot do anything about it because your failure is an internal disease. Your companies are based on Taylor's principles. Worse, your heads are Taylorized, too."

Wow! I didn't like reading that we would lose at anything, and I sure didn't like his comment about our heads being Taylorized. Who in the hell was Konosuke Matsushita to make such statements? He sure got my attention, so I read on. To my surprise, I found that many of the things that he was saying made sense to me. He believed that the American way of doing business was based on bosses doing all of the thinking and workers doing all of the actual work. He saw us advocating a complete separation between thinkers and doers. The assertion sounded reasonable; that was the way it was in most of my early jobs.

Matsushita also spoke about the role of management in the United States, stating that their primary purpose was to transfer the leaders' ideas to the workers' heads so they could effectively complete the work. He believed that in Japan, management practices were not limited by the principles introduced by Taylor: the Japanese understood that business had become extremely complex, and for businesses to prosper in an environment filled with risk and intense competition, their management practices had to change. They realized that even the brightest leaders in business were unable to adequately face these new challenges alone. Only the combined efforts of all team members—leaders, management, and workers—all working together would allow a company to flourish in the new world of industry. The Japanese had one definite advantage: they knew little of Taylor's principles and, therefore, didn't have to unlearn any detrimental Taylorisms.

Before I completely wrote off Matsushita's critique, I decided to learn a little more about Taylor.

Here's what I found. Fredrick Winslow Taylor was credited in the early 1900s for creating what he called "scientific management." His principles of leadership revolutionized the world of industry in the United States. At the beginning of the twentieth century, we were changing from a largely agricultural country to an industrial country. After Taylor introduced his principles of leadership, he was acknowledged by much of the industrial world as the reason that the United States emerged as a world leader in industry. To be fair, his principles have also been blamed for dehumanizing factories and work environments, and for creating separation between leaders and workers. Taylor believed that "captains of industry are born, not made," and he promoted the idea of planning separate from execution.

It is important to note here that Taylor's principles were being applied to a work force that was largely made up of men coming from an agricultural background. Many were immigrants who could not speak English, and most had very little formal education and even less understanding of how to work in a mechanized environment. Because of the available labor force, Taylor's principles of leadership (in which only leaders were capable of thinking and making decisions) worked, inasmuch as they increased worker productivity at that time.

Experiencing Taylorism

Matsushita could have mentioned that many US families were also Taylorized. Many of Taylor's principles were adapted into the parenting methods during that era. Dads did the thinking, and the rest of the family implemented his decisions. Eventually, this evolved into dads and moms doing the decision making jointly, with the children being told what to do and what not to do. (Frequently, without being able to ask "Why?") For me, this sounded a little too familiar. My dad's leadership style as a parent was very close to Taylorism: "Do what I tell you, when and how I tell you to do it." Now that I think about it, the management style in the Chicago factories where I worked was much the same. I was hired, I was told exactly what to do (many times without really understanding why I was doing it), and I was told that I had to do it the way they taught me or I would be fired. I was also told that if I didn't like it, I should quit because there were many other people waiting to do the work without asking questions.

I am sure that you can see the problems that such an environment created for me. Remember, I am the "Why?" guy. I was constantly looking for better ways to do things, and I wanted to know why it was necessary for me to do it their way, especially if I thought I knew a better way. These thoughts caused me a great deal of grief and unhappiness. It was dehumanizing for me!

Change in Business and Government

Many businesses and government agencies that operated under the

Taylor model have recognized that they must change if they want to succeed.

A notable example is General Motors.

For many years, General Motors was recognized as the biggest, most profitable company in the world. In 1970, GM was in a transition period; most of its leaders were rapidly reaching retirement age. To insure that GM continued as a world automotive leader, the retiring leaders decided to record why they felt GM had been so successful for so many years. Here are the seven conditions that GM leaders identified as being the most important to the past success (and critical to the future success) of the company:

1. GM is in the business of making money, not cars.
2. Success comes not from technological leadership, but from having the resources to quickly adopt innovations successfully introduced by others.
3. Styling is more important than quality.
4. The US car market is isolated from the world.
5. Energy will always be cheap and abundant.
6. Government is our enemy and cannot be trusted.
7. Management should come from within to avoid contamination from outside thinking.

Wow! I encourage you to reread these seven conditions, and keep in mind that these guidelines were intended to secure the company's position as a world leader in future years. Reading this today is almost comical. It is hard to believe that one of the greatest companies in the world was governed by people who believed that doing what they had always done, instead of changing with a changing world, would keep the company in the lead. Sounds a little Taylorized!

You'll not be surprised to hear that these guidelines failed to result in innovation or profitability. According to the Automotive Data Center, GM had 48.3 percent of the US sales in 1960, compared to 7.7 percent sales of imported cars. By 1990, GM's US market share had fallen to 35.2 percent, compared to 29.1 percent sales of imported cars. By 2009,

GM possessed only 19.5 percent of the market share, whereas 49.5 percent of all cars sold in the United States were imported. Ironically, a large number of those cars came from Japan, home of Matsushita. Many of the problems that GM's leaders experienced are a direct result of its leadership practices. But at long last, they too are changing. Why? To survive! They have learned that to survive they must function as a team comprised of both leaders and workers and rid themselves of the separation caused by Taylorism. Taylor's scientific management principles created separation between bosses and workers, separation between parents and children, and separation between coaches and players. Separation, in turn, creates teams that focus on their differences rather than their sameness; eventually, the teams become divided. The C&C model of leadership served us well for many decades. However, there have been constant changes away from this style because it is no longer producing the desired results.

We are in a transformation period, changing the way that people interact in businesses, in government, in families, and in sports. We are moving into a more interactive model of leadership, a model that recognizes that all members of a team are capable of contributing more than just their hard work. All are capable of contributing their ideas, and that dynamic can lead to leaders making Even Better decisions. Change is inevitable and will continue within all of our teams.

Coaching Hint

We see business teams, government teams, family teams, and sports teams fail every day because they refuse to change. Don't let the failure to change destroy your teams. Are your teams open to change?

Change in Thinking: Scarcity to Abundance

Another major change that is paralleling the changes in leadership style is the change in the way that many of us think, from one of scarcity to one of abundance. We have all heard of the glass half-full/half-empty way of thinking: optimists see the glass as half-full, while pessimists see it as half-empty. Why? Why are some people almost always optimistic, like Pollyanna, while so many others are pessimistic and negative in their thoughts and actions? Why is this important? Our basic beliefs determine how we live our lives; these same beliefs can also determine the success or failure of our teams. I believe that there is a correlation between pessimistic (half-empty) thinking and scarcity thinking. I also believe that there is a correlation between optimistic (half-full) thinking and abundance thinking. Keep your listening open.

Scarcity thinking is the belief that there is only so much of something to go around. Examples of scarcity thinking include "If you get it, I get less (or I don't get any)," or "The more I get, the less you get," or "If you win, I lose!" These thoughts may have come out of the Great Depression, when there was a scarcity of food, money, and jobs for many people.

My dad lived through the Great Depression, and I vividly remember his many lectures about money: "Money doesn't grow on trees." "A fool and his money are soon parted." "A penny saved is a penny earned." "You must save your money because tomorrow there may not be any more for you." Scarcity, scarcity, scarcity.

I also remember spending summers on my uncle's farm, where I learned more about scarcity at the dinner table. I was the smallest person at the table, with three older cousins and my aunt and uncle. When we were ready to start eating, the biggest, most aggressive people at the table got to the meat first. I got what was left. What I learned from this experience was that the more they took, the less there was for me. I quickly learned about scarcity thinking.

Scarcity thinking can also be developed in business, in sports, in family teams, and even in government teams by creating unhealthy competition between team members. When there is internal competition between team members, there is always a chance that some will feel like they have lost while others will feel like they have won, creating a win/loss situation. One result of win/lose situations is scarcity thinking; this can cause separation among team members. (Team building is about bringing people together, not creating separation.)

A common example of unhealthy internal competition among team members can be found in many car dealerships. Many leaders encourage their salespeople to compete against each other to increase car sales. There is a long-accepted belief that internal competition will increase sales. Rewards and acknowledgments are offered to those salespeople who sell the most cars, such as trips to the Bahamas. These trips are intended to motivate the sales force to sell more cars. Makes sense, right?

Let's look a little closer. Most of the time, in this kind of competition, the winner is predictable. The same two or three people always seem to win, year after year. At the opposite end of that spectrum, the same two or three people are almost always finishing last. In addition to these two extreme ends, there is a middle group of people who are just there, not excelling, not doing poorly, just there. Have you noticed this type of grouping in your teams: a few very successful people, a few not very successful people, and the rest somewhere in the middle? Keep your listening open. Think about it.

Let's look a little closer at the car dealership and see how this kind of competitive environment impacts teamwork. After a few contests where the results are about the same, the lowest and middle producers have very little incentive to compete. The top producers become even stronger, grow more aggressive, and continue to gather their rewards, which separates them from the other team members.

Eventually the others—less fortunate, less capable, or less trained—may even resent the winners. What happens next is predictable: anger, blame, resentment, and bruised self-esteem, which causes even greater team separation. Unhealthy internal competition creates winners and losers; it creates failure, and no one likes to lose or to fail. When you have unhealthy competition within a team, only a few members will win, while most members of the team lose. Another undesirable result is the top salespeople can't understand why the other team members don't do well and become judgmental and critical of those who are less successful. Separation continues when the daily, weekly, and monthly reviews of individual productivity point out who's winning and who's losing.

In this unhealthy competitive environment, the most productive salespeople may also become protective of their customers and protect their secrets; they do not share their methods for success. If you are repeatedly the top salesperson who goes to the Bahamas every year, are you going to share your expertise with other team members? Are you going to assist them, encourage them, and train them, knowing that there is a possibility that someone else may eventually win the Bahamas bonus rather than you? (This is scarcity thinking.) Probably not! Some people will even sabotage the sales of others just to win. This type of unhealthy competitive environment is not comfortable for any of the sales force or for their customers. All of this is about scarcity, and none of it improves the productivity of individuals or their teams.

Abundance Thinking: You Win, I Win, We All Win

Successful leaders are beginning to look at the bigger picture—how can everyone win: the owner, the sales force, and the customer? They are learning that both individual and team goals can be achieved without creating losers. When a team focuses on improving by helping each other rather than beating each other, the team and each individual will become more productive. Many dealerships are creating new incentive plans that reward the entire team when they reach their desired sales goals. The only competition is for each individual and the entire team to exceed their past performances (healthy competition). In addition to the sales team, clerical workers and service workers are being recognized for contributing to the total team win (members of the extended team). Instead of one person or a single group of people going to the Bahamas for a week, everyone in the dealership is included in some type of collective team reward.

In the car dealership sales model, when successful leaders reward team efforts, rather than individual efforts, total productivity increases. Top salespeople begin to help the middle and bottom salespeople. They will assist, encourage, and teach others their skills and secrets for success, because they know that for them to win, all team members must contribute to the team's efforts.

This model is based on abundance thinking. There is enough for everyone to win; no one has to be a loser. If I help them, they will help me, and we will all benefit.

Abundance thinking applies to every team. Abundance thinking leads to the belief that there is plenty of everything to go around for you, for me, for everyone. Enough profits, enough love, enough money, enough success, enough fame, enough power, and enough recognition for everyone. Leaders and members from all types of teams are beginning to realize that both individual and team goals can be achieved without creating losers. When a team focuses on improving by training every team member to help each other succeed, everyone will get better. When leaders reward team efforts, rather than individual efforts, team and individual productivity increases. Team goals are developed where rewards and acknowledgments are made only when team goals are reached. Leaders also acknowledge and reward team members for their efforts to assist others and for their efforts at teamwork, which results in the most experienced team members helping those who are less successful.

Scarcity/Abundance Thinking in Families

Let's look at a family where children compete against each other for their parents' support and affection. This type of unhealthy competition can create the belief that there is only so much love to go around, which implies that there are winners and losers. Parents can also develop scarcity thinking: one parent may say to the other, "The kids always come first; you give them more attention than you do to me." When this kind of unhealthy internal competitive environment exists, team members compete for attention; they undermine, accuse, rebel, blame, and some may even quit trying. Abundance thinking creates an environment where there is plenty of love and affection for everyone; there is no desire or need to compete with each other for attention or acceptance.

Scarcity/Abundance Thinking in Education

Let's look at the world of education; many students have been subjected to scarcity thinking since their very first years in school. Some teachers grade on what is called the Bell Curve. The Bell Curve roughly states that in a normal classroom of students, the A students will be balanced with a few F students; a few D students will be balanced with a few B students; and the middle group will be made up of average students with C grades. This philosophy can create unhealthy competition between students, who develop the belief that there are winners and losers. Why can't there be a class where every student earns an A or B? We know from the car dealership example that unhealthy competition among team members does not accomplish the desired results. I believe that the same undesirable results can happen when students compete with one another for grades: it creates winners and losers and scarcity thinking!

Some educators are experimenting with an entirely different grading system, treating a class of students as if they were a team, with the primary goal of everyone helping each other to succeed. One of the more progressive ideas is to have only one student's final exam grade count for everyone in the class. The selection of that exam is not made until everyone has competed their test. That's an interesting idea, right? If you were an A or B student in that class, I bet your hands would be sweating; no doubt you would think, *What happens if one of the D or F students' exam is selected? I'm going to end up with a D or F! What about my chances to get into medical school?* Or, if you were like I was in high school, then you may be thinking, *Great! If they choose one of the smart A or B students' exams, I'm good!*

In most traditional classrooms, the A students get their As, many times without a great deal of effort. The D and F students may just not care or just coast, while the remaining students fall somewhere in the middle, struggling, trying, and many times not really motivated to get good grades. Have you noticed the similarity to the sales team at the car dealership? There is good news from the experimental classes: the A and B students begin to help the D and F students, as well as the middle group of C students. Every single student realizes that his or her test might be the one chosen and that grade will be given to everyone in the class. No one wants to mess up and cause everyone else to get a low grade! So the A and B students not only have to learn the material that they will be tested on, they must also learn how to teach it. Not only must they teach it, they must learn how to teach it to people less motivated or less capable academically than themselves: they are forced to put themselves in the shoes of their classmates.

Take a few minutes to think about the dynamics of this experiment and the potential for growth and development for all of the students in the class. Think of the professional and personal growth for teachers and parents. In an experimental class of this type, everyone is viewed as necessary for the class to succeed. Some in the class will be peacemakers, some cheerleaders, some class clowns committed to keep everyone relaxed and loose, some enforcers, and some tutors, with each of their roles dynamic and constantly changing. This experimental class creates a challenge for everyone, one that requires all team members, with all levels of desire, capability, and commitment, to work together. This is a challenge that leads to the personal growth and development of each and every individual in the class. Quite an experiment! Yes, times are changing.

Coaching Hint

Before you try to locate the research from these experimental classes, you should know it was not the results that helped me to change my thinking, it was the concept. It gave me a whole new way to approach teamwork. Spend some time thinking about how the ideas from this example can be applied to one of your teams.

Abundance Thinking in Competitive Gymnastics

As a gymnastics coach, I was always amazed at how the gymnasts on my teams would constantly work together and help each other. It took doing this research for me to fully understand the concept of abundance thinking. My gymnasts would help each other, even if it meant that the person they helped might later beat them for a position on the team. This prompts the question, why? Why would anyone help someone that may eventually take his position on the team?

On a men's gymnastics team, there are six events: floor exercise, pommel horse, rings, vaulting, parallel bars, and high bar. When I was coaching gymnastics at the University of Oregon, the NCAA rules allowed only six competitors in each event. Some team members would compete on only one event, while others competed on two or three events, and some competed on all six events. The goal of every athlete was to be one of the top six performers in an event and compete in a meet. Each day, there were twenty-five to thirty gymnasts working out, training to make the team. For each of the six events, there were usually nine or ten gymnasts who were competing for one of the six positions. Gymnastics is an individual sport, requiring lots of one-on-one coaching attention with each athlete. It's a rarity when everyone does drills or simultaneously works together as a unit. This means that in a four- or five-hour workout, there is a limited amount of time that the coaches can spend with each gymnast. So who does the necessary one-on-one coaching? You guessed it: the gymnasts. They coach each other. They spot for each other, assist each other, evaluate each other's performances, and share ideas with each other. We are back to that question again: Why? Why would anyone help someone else when his help may result in the other person taking his position on the team? "Why should I help you (or you help me) if as a result of this help, you win and I lose (or I win and you lose)?"

Herein lies the answer to teams that work together and win together. It's about you win and I win; we each move toward our primary personal goals to become Even Better, to become the best we can become. It's about the bigger win. It's about abundance thinking.

Nobody has stated this idea better than the iconic basketball coach from UCLA, John Wooden, when he said, "Winning is the peace of mind which is a direct result of self-satisfaction in knowing you did your best to become the best that you are capable of becoming."

What will you take away from the car dealership example of scarcity and unhealthy internal competition? What will you take away from the example of the gymnastics team that believed in abundance thinking and understood that by helping each other, they were also helping themselves and the team to become Even Better? What will you take away from the progressive classroom experiment? What will you do?

Chapter 4
Two Different Teams, Two Different Results

During my coaching years at the University of Oregon, my wife and I were also parenting two exceptional teenage daughters. It was always a mystery to me how I could go into the gym six days a week with twenty-five to thirty young men and make almost unreasonable (some would say completely unreasonable) demands of them physically, emotionally, and intellectually, and they would respond with outstanding performances in competition, in the classroom, and in the community. At home, however, it was a different story.

Why? Why was I successful as a gymnastics coach but felt much less successful as a parent?

I remember going into the gym and trying all of these different ways to get the gymnasts to be more motivated, to be more inspired, to be more productive, to work harder, to win, and it worked. I also remember going home equally committed to having a winning family team and highly productive teenage daughters, and it didn't quite work the same way. Years later, as I was doing the research for *Even Better!*, I finally began to understand why these entirely different scenarios occurred.

Looking back, I remembered that before athletes became members of our gymnastics team, I would visit their homes, spending time with them and their families. While in their homes, I would talk about my passion and enthusiasm for the University of Oregon and our gymnastics program. I shared my dream for Oregon gymnastics with them. I would talk about the beautiful campus, the outstanding academics, the community, the state, the ocean, the rivers, the mountains, and the wonderful environment in which they could train, study, and live. I spoke about how they could reach their personal dreams and goals in gymnastics and academics if they chose to become Oregon gymnasts.

In addition to sharing my dreams and information about the university, I told them that I would help them to become the best students and gymnasts possible and become positive, contributing members of the community. I also told them that we practiced six days a week and shared, in detail, what I expected from them as Oregon gymnasts.

Soon after my visit with the gymnast and his family, he would make his decision: He would say, "Yes, that's a great place for me to go to school and to live the next few years," or "Yes, I agree and want Bill Ballester to be my coach, because I believe he and the University of Oregon can help me to realize my dreams." Or he would say, "No, I don't want to become an Oregon gymnast, and I want to go somewhere else to train and to live," or "No, having Bill Ballester for my coach is not what I want. I have different dreams and goals. I don't think Oregon is the right place for me."

When a gymnast chose Oregon and agreed to be coached by me, we had a shared dream; we each agreed to make a commitment to work together and make our dreams a reality. The gymnast made an informed choice. We began our relationship with a mutual understanding of each other's expectations, and we had a common dream that we agreed to.

Guess what? I didn't share my dream for our family with my children. I assumed that they knew my dream was to see them well, happy, and successful at everything they attempted. I never shared that dream with them. I never talked about how I was committed to their growth and development, and how I would help them to accomplish their personal dreams and goals. We never discussed that by being a contributing and vital part of our family team, they could also achieve their personal dreams and goals. I never asked them if I could be their coach, their father, their mentor, or anything else. They were simply told what they were expected to do and how it was to be done. (Echoes of Taylorism, right?)

There were two major differences between my family team and the gymnastics team: Every gymnast knew the dream and goals of the team, and they had a choice: they could decide whether they wanted to become members of the team or not. The girls did not know the dream or the family goals, and they were not given a chance to choose their family team or their parents. They were not given a choice. From my experience as a dad and as a coach, I have learned that all teams, even family teams, require a clearly stated and commonly understood dream to be successful, and all members must have the option to accept or reject the dream.

When was the last time you shared your dream with your family? When was the last time you and your family talked together about the family dream? "Never" would have been my answer when my daughters were growing up. I simply did not understand the value or the necessity of having a clear, easily understood dream and sharing it with my family.

If your answer is never, I encourage you to spend some time to become very clear about your dream for your family and then share it with them.

Winners are more willing to pay the price when the coach becomes more skilled at painting vivid pictures of the desired end results or benefits. Putting the why *into our communication brings about incredible performances from our players.*

—*Vince Lombardi*

The Dream

You may be thinking, "Coach, I understand what you're saying, but this dream thing is still a little unclear. I'm not even sure what my dream is. Where can I find it?" Good question. Take a few minutes, sit back, and do a little daydreaming. A good place to start is in your heart. Do you remember when you and your partner first began to think about becoming a couple? What were your hopes, desires, and desired results? It is those feelings and those thoughts that formed your dream and became the common purpose to become a team.

This is where you find your dreams.

If you have children, do you remember when you held your child for the first time and the love that you felt? This is where dreams begin, dreams of that child being happy, healthy, and successful (maybe someday becoming a doctor, a fireman, a nurse, the president of the United States).

This is where you find your dreams.

Do you remember how you felt when you got your current job? Do you remember thinking how you were going to accomplish great things in your new position and how you were going to change things for the better? Relive that first day when you went home and told your loved ones about your new job. Think about how happy and excited you were.

This is where you find your dreams.

Once you have found your dream, write it on paper and begin to share it with your family. If your dream is for them to be happy, healthy, honest, self-supporting, confident, and successful, share those thoughts with them and then ask them if they want these same things for themselves. Remember, you are simply sharing your dream for them and for your family; share it from your heart, not from your head. Ask them for their ideas; work together to create a family dream that everyone can agree to support. When you have a dream, ask them if they will *also* agree to work together as a team to make these family dreams a reality.

I have asked audiences made up of coaches and business and government leaders the "When was the last time ..." questions about their work teams. I ask them, "When was the last time you had a conversation with your work team about your personal dream and goals for the team? When was the last time you discussed these thoughts with your team members?" Unfortunately, the answers to these questions are usually similar to those given about the family team: "Not in a long time" or "Never."

Dreams for businesses and for government teams are sometimes less obvious, harder to understand, and easier to forget. It is when dreams are unclear, not understood, or not agreed upon that teams become less productive, falter, frequently separate, and finally stop functioning.

A dream requires continuous review and updating, with frequent discussion with all members of the team. Constantly speaking about and repeating our dreams to team members also serves as a reminder for each of us as to why the team exists. These reminders will provide additional motivation for everyone to work together as a cohesive team. Constantly repeating a team's purpose and its desired results is an important responsibility of a successful team leader, because it provides clarity and a common team focus.

Coaching Hint

All successful teams start with a common dream and an agreement.
Without agreement, there is no commitment.
Without commitment, there is no action.
Without action, there is no productivity.
Without productivity, there is no winning and no success.

Coaching Hint

When you tell others your dreams, some will not share your enthusiasm or excitement. They may not be interested to hear what you have to say. Others may not be supportive, and some may even try to discourage you. Remember, it is your dream; hold on to your dream and keep sharing it until you find others who want the same things.

I also learned from these two different teams that all agreements are not equal. There is a direct correlation between levels of agreement and the success or lack of success on all teams. The gymnasts made agreements at the highest level, based on their understanding of the dream and the common goals that we all shared. My daughters did not understand the dreams or goals for them and our family and their levels of agreement and support for the dream—at the time—did not create the necessary levels of commitment to make the dream for the family a reality.

Agreements

When human beings interact, there is usually some type of communication, some sort of dialogue, some form of exchange of information. Regardless of the subject or the circumstances, each person involved in the interaction forms some sort of opinion about this information. These opinions range from total agreement to total disagreement and all levels in between. For people to successfully interact together as a team, there must be high levels of agreement. By understanding the different levels of agreement and disagreement, leaders have another valuable tool that helps them to make Even Better decisions for their teams and their team members.

Levels of Agreement

(I think of 10 as a perfect score.)

10. Agreement: "It's as good as done." "Whatever it takes!"

9. Qualified Yes: "Let's do it, unless …"

8. Buying In: "That's a good idea." "How about this?"

7. Establishing Value: "That's a good idea."

6. Open to the Idea: "That's an idea. Let's talk about it."

Levels of Disagreement

5. Neutral/Ignorance: "I don't know and I don't care."

4. Apathy: "I don't care."

3. Nonactive Resistance: The Look; "Nothing." "Fine." Silence.

2. Active Resistance: "No, I disagree!"

1. Physical Aggression: Fighting.

0. Disagreement: War, killing, destruction.

Let's break down each of these levels to better understand their differences. I will start at the least desirable and most destructive levels of disagreement.

Levels of Disagreement

Level 0: Disagreement (War, killing, destruction)

This is where people disagree so much that they are willing to kill one another in their efforts to be right; they are willing to die because of their disagreements. This level of disagreement has happened repeatedly in history, demonstrated by wars, including civil wars within countries. Survival in this type of world is questionable; it is not the kind of world that most of us want to create or endure.

Level 1: Physical Aggression (Fighting)

When I was a teenager growing up near Chicago, this level of disagreement was how my friends and I would resolve many of our disagreements. Two or more of us would have a disagreement about something, and that disagreement soon led to physical aggression. We would fight, hit, kick, scratch, bite, or whatever seemed necessary at the time. Each of us was willing to fight for what we felt was right (or to avoid admitting that we might be wrong).

This is not limited by sex or age. Watch a couple of two-year-olds fighting over a toy, each insisting that the toy is his or her own. This disagreement frequently moves to Level 1, involving hitting and lots of crying. You can see this level of disagreement in every society and at every age. Such disagreements are caused by our convictions that "We are right and they are wrong."

Level 2: Active Resistance ("No, I disagree!")

This level is even more prevalent and frequently leads to Level 1 (and potentially back down to Level 0). Arguing comes in many forms, ranging from outright yelling to toe-to-toe, in-your-face posturing. Frequently at this level, names are called and harsh words are spoken that create separation and lasting scars that may eventually destroy the team.

Level 3: Nonactive Resistance (The Look)

You know what "the look" is, don't you? This is the look that I frequently got from my daughters during their teenage years when I told them what I expected from them. It is the look that you occasionally give to your boss or that your employees occasionally give to you. You know, the look! The look usually comes from someone who wants to avoid an outright Level 2 argument, perhaps out of the fear of reprisal. Sometimes we use the look with our spouse or partner, just to avoid an argument (or worse, a Level 1 fight). The look is a comparatively subtle action.

You immediately knew what I meant when I said the look, because it is widely used. The look can say a lot, depending on who gives it. It can say, "I don't agree with you," "I don't believe you," "I don't want to do what you want me to do," "I'm not confident in your decision." At the very least, the look says, "I'm not committed to your idea, and I do not agree." Yes, we all know the look. In terms of teamwork, Level 3 may be the most destructive, because it doesn't really convey any useful information. Do they care? Are they angry? Do they disagree? Are they disappointed? Do they lack the courage to address the problem?

Level 4: Apathy ("I don't care.")

Level 4 often takes the form of a blank stare or silence. It is very closely related to Level 3 and the look. However, disagreement is not expressed, simply apathy: "I don't disagree, I don't agree, I just don't care." Levels 3 and 4 frequently overlap, and it takes keen perception to distinguish the two. Distinguishing the subtle difference between them is not important. What is important is that you recognize the lack of agreement intended.

Level 5: Neutral/Ignorance ("I don't know, and I don't care.")

Level 5 is being neutral or just not understanding enough to have an opinion. "I don't agree, I don't disagree; I may care, but I just don't understand." At this level, team members still lack interest in participating together as a team.

With those nonproductive levels behind us, we can now talk about levels of agreement that will bring teams together.

Levels of Agreement

Level 6: Open to the Idea ("That's an idea. Let's talk about it.")

As we progress to a Level 6 agreement, we are now keeping our minds open to possibility. We are going in a direction that is useful and necessary for teamwork and higher levels of productivity. Level 6 is when team members are willing to consider the possibility that an idea has value: they are open to listen, and they are coachable. Teams that are coachable rapidly move to the next levels of agreement.

Level 7: Establishing Value ("That's a good idea.")

This is the starting point for building a winning team: getting team members to agree to what is suggested or proposed as a "good idea." This is one of the greatest challenges for all team leaders. From Level 7, motivating team members to higher levels of agreement becomes much easier.

Level 8: Buying In ("That's a good idea. How about this?")

Level 8 is when team members have bought into an idea and are excited enough to want to improve the outcome by adding their own thoughts and ideas. This is a great place for a team leader and the team members to find themselves. However, it can also be a level of potential problems if the leader is not open to really listen (with an open mind) to the thoughts and ideas from all team members (even the bad ideas). Leaders must be willing to accept the possibility that a team member may have an idea that—when combined with their own idea—may be Even Better.

Many traditional leaders have problems with this level. They have been trained that the team leader has the sole responsibility to provide all of the answers. Others believe their position as experienced team leaders automatically means their ideas are the best and need no further refinement. In contrast, leaders who encourage open dialogue and truly want to see their team members grow personally and develop their skill levels will provide opportunities for all members to speak their mind and offer their suggestions. Leaders who are not open to listen to their team members frequently cause their teams to regress back to Levels 4 and 5.

Level 9: Qualified Yes ("Let's do it, unless ...")

A Level 9 agreement is the level at which many of us live. It's a very useful level, but it isn't a Level 10. Level 9 is okay, and it is certainly better than the other levels, but there is an "unless" attached to the agreement. This "unless" frequently sounds like this:

Person 1: "Let's go fishing next week."

Person 2: "Okay, let's do it unless it rains." (Or "Unless I have to do work around the house," or "Unless the kids want to go to the park.")

A football coach tells one of his players, "The team needs you to catch this ball for a ten-yard gain; will you do it?"

The player responds, "I sure will, Coach, unless I get knocked down. (Or "Unless someone else catches it," or "Unless the quarterback doesn't throw the ball well.")

Level 9 agreements indicate we are in agreement, we are going in the same direction, we want the same outcomes, and we will do it ... unless.

Level 10: Agreement (Full Commitment)

Level 10 may be the easiest level to understand and recognize: you make agreements and you keep them. You remove the "unless" from Level 9. Level 10 agreements create teams and team members who do *what* they say they will do, *when* they say they will do it, and *how* they say they will do it. The ultimate goal of all leaders is to reach a Level 10 commitment with everyone on the team.

Family Agreements

Keeping agreements with your children is extremely important for continued family growth and development. Pretend for a moment that you are the father of a three-year-old girl. As you are heading off to work on a Monday morning, your daughter says, "Daddy, will you read me a story? Please, please, read me a story!" You quickly respond, "I can't read to you right now, but when I get home tonight, I will read you a story." You give her a hug and leave for work. Now, let's say it turns out to be one of those days, where everything goes wrong and you come home with an intense headache and a briefcase full of work that must be completed by the next morning.

Guess what? As you open the door, wanting to unwind for a short period of time, your daughter immediately grabs your leg, looks up, and says, "Daddy, please read me my story now; you said you would when you got home from work." Like many parents, you may launch into an explanation about how hard your day at work was, and you go on about the headache you have and the work you have to complete that night. Then you promise to read the story tomorrow morning. Does any of this sound familiar? Do you think that your three-year-old daughter cares about your excuses, about your workload, about your responsibilities? Do you think she really cares if your reasons for not reading the story are true or accurate? Of course not! She only wants you to read her a story.

Many of us go through life making agreements and then breaking them because we feel that we have good reasons. I have learned that it doesn't make any difference why you break agreements; the results are the same: there is a loss of trust. People will eventually not trust you to do what you agree to do; they will no longer agree to do things with you. This may help us to understand why our children, when they become teenagers, frequently don't keep their agreements with us. Think about it.

Keeping Your Agreements

Sometimes people have every intention of keeping their agreements at a Level 10 but fail to do so. For instance, you and I agree to meet for lunch next week to talk more about winning and teamwork. We have each agreed that lunch would be a good idea, and we are both excited about doing it, so we set up our lunch meeting for next Wednesday at 12:00. Next Wednesday, I show up at McDonald's and you show up at Wendy's. We both forgot to choose where we were to meet; however, regardless of the reason, it is still a broken agreement. When we break agreements, there are always natural ramifications.

Coaching Hint

When you make agreements, be very clear about what level of agreement you are asking for and what level of agreement your team members are willing to give. When seeking agreement, always includes the **5 Ws: WHY** are we doing it? **WHAT** are we going to do? **WHERE** are we going to do it? **WHO** is going to do it? **WHEN** are we going to do it, and **when** are we going to finish it? Leaders who follow these steps rarely experience people breaking their agreements due to a lack of understanding or confusion. When this process is followed, agreements are more apt to reach Level 10.

Let's take a closer look at some of these natural ramifications: We agree to meet again next Wednesday at noon at Wendy's; this time we are both clear about where we will meet. Once again, I don't show up. You are sitting there in Wendy's, waiting. What's going on in your mind? You may be thinking, *We covered the 5 Ws, so I am sure I got the time and the place right.* Next you think, *It's ten after twelve. Bill is late. He must have been held up.* Another five minutes go by, and you may be thinking, *I wonder if Bill got into some sort of accident; maybe he's held up in traffic. Should I go ahead and order?* Fifteen more minutes roll off the clock: *If Bill really cared, he would be here or at least call me.* After a whole hour passes, you think, *Wow, Bill must have thought this was not very important or he would have called me.*

Later that day I call you, apologizing and explaining that I had an emergency at the office and just couldn't make it for lunch. I suggest that we plan to meet again the following Wednesday. Once again, we go over the 5 Ws to make sure we both understand. Because I broke our last lunch agreement, I offer to buy lunch the next week.

Next Wednesday arrives, and guess what? The same thing happens again. I don't show up or call. This week, the internal conversations you have while you are waiting for me come at a much faster rate; you may be thinking that I don't really care about you. You may also have some internal anger directed toward me. Is that pretty close to being right? I call again that afternoon, explaining that I had car trouble and just couldn't make it to our lunch meeting. Now consider how you would react to my excuses for not keeping my agreement with you. Does it make any difference if my excuses are valid or reasonable?

Would you be willing to agree to meet me again for lunch? How do you feel about this? You may be a little hesitant; you may consider saying no. You may look back at the last three weeks and remember how you felt as you were waiting alone—wondering, worrying, feeling somewhat foolish—each time, sitting there waiting for almost an hour. You may say to yourself, "If I agree again, will this be the fourth week that Bill doesn't show up?" You may also be thinking about those other Wednesdays when you declined invitations for lunch with friends, because you had agreed to meet with me and you felt obligated to keep our agreements.

The point of this lengthy story is to be very clear about what happens when people break their agreements. Are we bad people when we break our agreements? I prefer to not use the words "good" or "bad," because it requires me to make a judgment. However, I do believe when anyone breaks an agreement, there are always natural ramifications. One of the most destructive ramifications is a loss of trust. Without trust, relationships fail. *All successful relationships are based on mutual trust.*

I can almost hear you thinking, *How do you deal with agreements that you make and can't keep?* Good question.

This is an easy one: Change it before you break it!

If you and I make a Level 10 agreement and I can't keep it, it is up to me to tell you that I can't keep my agreement with you. This must be done before the time that we agreed upon. Now we are changing our agreement, not breaking it. Sometimes, the changing of an agreement is necessary.

Let's agree to try another lunch meeting; we are clear about all of the details. However, once again I have a problem; I call you before our agreed-upon time to inform you that I can't make it. Now we each have new choices to consider. I can request another day or perhaps even another time. We can discuss the options and come to a new agreement (or maybe even agree to not meet at all). What is important is that we come to a new agreement before breaking the original one.

What happens when we make agreements and frequently change them? Another good question. When people constantly change their agreements, they experience many of the same ramifications as if they had broken them. Loss of trust becomes an issue and eventually leads to having everything they say or do questioned. Others may also stop making agreements with them and ultimately begin to question the value of the relationship.

Changing agreements is sometimes necessary; however, if we are very careful to consider exactly what we are agreeing to, and our intention is to keep all of our agreements at a Level 10, we will dramatically reduce the number of times that we must change them.

Part Two:
A Leadership Model for Winning Teams

The Nine Principles of Winning Teams is a leadership model for developing and maintaining winning teams, taken from research with highly successful coaches from the world of sports, confirmed by leaders from business and government, and echoed by successful parents.

Larry Spencer and I had many long conversations about sports; we often talked about coaches and their players. Our conversations generated many unanswered questions. We wanted to know why some coaches always seemed to win while others did not. We wondered if there were similarities among all highly successful coaches and the way they interacted with their players. We decided to try to find the answers to these and other questions by interviewing successful coaches: coaches of young children, coaches of high school and college athletes, and coaches of professional athletes. We interviewed both male and female coaches, representing a variety of different leadership (coaching) styles from many different parts of the country. Our research was designed to identify common elements used by these winning coaches.

We did not use a traditional question-and-answer interview. Instead, we designed the interview to be open and free flowing, allowing coaches to openly express themselves without being confined to answering specific questions. As we moved forward with our interviews, we began to hear similarities in their responses—not the same words, and not necessarily the same acknowledged concepts or techniques, but similar thoughts and similar reactions to particular situations. Some coaches could clearly articulate why and how they were able to create winning teams; other coaches were not able to explain why their teams always seemed to win, but they all understood that if they tried something that didn't work, they let it go and changed what they were doing until they found something that did work. This provided us with one answer to our first question: Why do some coaches always seem to win while others do not? Winners don't continue to do things that don't work.

We also found the answer to our next question: Are there similarities among all highly successful coaches and the way they interact with their players? Yes, we learned that there are similar principles used by all winning coaches: those who coached professional teams, those who coached young children, and those who coached high school and university athletics. We also learned that these same principles worked with both male and female athletes of all ages.

Finding the answers to these questions led us to our next questions: Is it possible that the same principles used by winning coaches can be used with business leaders and their employees? Could we develop a leadership model taken from the world of sports and apply it to the world of business? We had taped each of the interviews, which became a wonderful source of information to revisit when we began to distill our research for the development of our leadership model. We call this model the Nine Principles for Winning Teams.

I acknowledge the following coaches who provided much of the initial information for developing the Nine Principles of Winning Teams. Among these highly successful coaches are icons from their respective sports, leaders, innovators, and even a few mavericks, each with one single thing in common: they were all consistent winners. I invite you to read through the list of names and take some time to learn more about their coaching careers and their lives.

John Wooden: Men's Basketball, *UCLA*
Pete Newell: Men's Basketball, *UC Berkeley*
Marv Harshman: Men's Basketball, *University of Washington*
Jerry Tarkanian: Men's Basketball, *University of Nevada at Las Vegas*

Lute Olson: Men's Basketball, *University of Arizona*

Linda Sharp: Women's Basketball, *University of Southern California*

Joan Bonvicini: Women's Basketball, *Long Beach State University*

Bob Boyd: Men's Basketball, *University of Southern California*

Morgan Wooten: Men's Basketball, *Dematha High School, Baltimore, Maryland*

Bill Walsh: NFL Football, *San Francisco 49ers*

Chris Gobrecht: Women's Basketball, *University of Washington*

Elwin Heiny: Women's Basketball, *University of Oregon*

Lou Campanelli: Men's Basketball, *UC Berkeley*

Bruce O'Neal: Men's Basketball, *University of Hawaii* and *Hawaii Volcanoes (CBA)*

Jim Harrick: Men's Basketball, *UCLA*

Laurel Tindall: Women's Gymnastics, *Seattle Pacific University*

Henretta Heiny: Women's Gymnastics, *University of Oregon*

Edwin Peery: Wrestling, *United States Naval Academy*

Ron Finley: Wrestling, *University of Oregon*

Dick Mulvihill: Men's and Women's Gymnastics, *The Gymnastics Academy, Eugene, Oregon*

Peter Kormann: Men's and Women's Gymnastics, *United States Naval Academy*

Newt Loken: Men's Gymnastics, *University of Michigan*

John Draghi: Men's Gymnastics, *Long Beach City College*

Dick Harter: Men's Professional Basketball, *Charlotte Hornets*

Rod Dedeaux: Men's Baseball, *University of Southern California*

John Scolinos: Men's Baseball, *Cal Poly Pomona*

Bobo Brayton: Men's Baseball, *Washington State University*

Norv Ritchey: Men's Baseball, *University of Oregon*

Judi Garman: Women's Softball, *Cal State Fullerton*

Gene Wettstone: Men's Gymnastics, *Penn State University*

Becky Sisley: Women's Softball, *University of Oregon*

Sid Gillman: NFL Football, *San Diego Chargers*

Don James: Football, *University of Washington*

Terry Donahue: Football, *UCLA*

Jack Patera: NFL Football, *Seattle Seahawks*

Len Casanova: Football, *University of Oregon*
Ken Morrow: Football, *Age Group, Eugene, Oregon*
Bill Dellinger: Men's Track and Field, *University of Oregon*
John Chaplain: Men's Track and Field, *University of Washington*
Bob Larson: Men's Track and Field, *UCLA*
Terry Crawford: Women's Track and Field, *University of Texas*
Bev Rouse: Women's Track and Field, *University of Arkansas*
Bev Kearney: Women's Track and Field, *University of Florida*
Stan Huntsman: Men's Track and Field, *University of Texas*
Tom Heinonen: Women's Track and Field, *University of Oregon*
Loren Seagraves: Women's Track and Field, *Louisiana State University*
Ted Banks: Men's Track and Field, *University of Texas at El Paso*
Ron Alice: Men's Track and Field, *Long Beach City College*
Linda Mulvihill: Men's and Women's Gymnastics, *The Gymnastics Academy, Eugene, Oregon*
Bill Bowerman: Men's Track and Field, *University of Oregon*
Don Robinson: Men's Gymnastics, *Arizona State University*
Bill Meade: Men's Gymnastics, *Southern Illinois University*
Dick Wolfe: Men's Gymnastics, *Cal State Fullerton*
Bobby Douglas: Wrestling, *Arizona State University*
Monte Nitzkowsky: Water Polo, *Long Beach City College*
Don Van Rossen: Men's and Women's Swimming, *University of Oregon*
Virginia Van Rossen: Men's and Women's Swimming, *University of Oregon*
Dick Erikson: Men's Rowing, *University of Washington*
Bob Ernst: Women's Rowing, *University of Washington*
Jim Verdieck: Men's Tennis, *University of Redlands*
Andre Deladrie: Men's and Women's Fencing, *United States Naval Academy*
Cliff McGrath: Men's Soccer, *Seattle Pacific University*
Bartlett Giamatti: President of Yale University, Commissioner of Major League Baseball

I also acknowledge and thank those many business, government, and family leaders who over the years have refined and defined this model so it can be effectively used by all teams.

The concept of modeling has always been a part of our lives; we all model the behavior of others. We often model our parents' behavior, and our children, in turn, model ours. We can also model the behavior of successful people when we choose a career. For example, if I wanted to become a doctor, I would model the behavior of already successful doctors. I would go to undergraduate school, get good grades, and then go on to medical school, where I would take classes that successful doctors had taken before me. If I could accurately and effectively model the methods through which someone else became a successful doctor, I would become a successful doctor. If I wanted to become a professional skier, I would watch what successful skiers do and attempt to emulate their moves and learn the methods that created their success.

Another example showing how an entire sport can be changed by modeling was the development of US men's gymnastics. When I began coaching gymnastics at the University of Oregon in the 1970s, the male gymnasts from Japan were the best in the world. At that time, I did not consciously understand the concept of modeling; however, along with many other American coaches, I began to evaluate films of the championship Japanese team members. We wanted to learn more about what they were doing and how they were doing it. Our intention was to train American gymnasts to develop the same skills and to master the same moves through the process of modeling.

Next, we invited a few of the Japanese gymnasts into our gyms to learn about their training habits and their way of thinking. With films to model and Japanese gymnasts guiding our efforts, American gymnasts were able to emulate and duplicate their skills. As a direct result of hard work and modeling the techniques and skills of the best in the world, we moved closer to our dream of being Olympic champions. A few years later, an American team beat the Japanese in international competition for the first time. I was given the opportunity to become a part of this success as the American coach and meet director for the competition at the University of Oregon.

In 1984, by adding a few of our own innovations and modeling the successful systems of many of the world's best gymnasts, the US men's gymnastics team became Olympic champions.

The Nine Principles of Winning Teams is a leadership model for all teams: sports, business, government, and family.

Part Three:

The Nine Principles of Winning Teams

A principle can be viewed as a basic truth, a standard to follow, a mode of action.

These principles are not a set of rules; they are not a list of "how tos"; they are not presented in any order of importance. Each is essential to winning and a reflection of what occurs within all successful teams. In addition to the nine principles, I have included many examples and stories that have helped me to better understand their meanings.

As you read each principle, continue to ask yourself "Why" and "How" questions.

Principle #1: The Double Win

The Double Win is the foundation principle for all successful teams. It is the basic belief that for a team to win, team leaders must invest in the growth and development of each team member. Their investment is rewarded with loyalty, commitment, teamwork, and higher levels of productivity, which translate into both individual and team success.

All teams, whether created by choice or by birth, benefit and prosper when the leaders are committed to each team member and willing to invest in their skill development and personal growth.

Family teams provide a good example of the Double Win. Most parents realize that they must spend meaningful time with their children, teaching them survival skills, social skills, values, discipline, and ultimately the skills necessary to become contributing members of society. The time and effort spent is an investment: not only in their children, but also in the family's future. When children are able to learn the many skills necessary to survive and excel, it becomes a win for the child and a win for the entire family.

In sports, effective coaches realize that for their teams to win, each individual player must also win. Winning requires the development of skills specific to each sport, and these skills require repetition; this repetition is called practice. Successful scholastic coaches also realize to win, their athletes must successfully perform in the classroom and in the community. This requires a different type of investment; it requires taking an interest in the backgrounds of their athletes: knowing where they were raised, knowing their families, knowing their lifestyle. They must also create personal relationships with their athletes: relationships that help them understand their players' personal dreams, goals, and commitment and desire to excel. As athletes develop and become more skilled at their sport and more skilled in their personal lives, they are rewarded with better personal performances. When the performance of each player improves, the team improves; the results: the team wins and each player wins.

The Double Win is the foundation principle for all teams: the greater the investment in the growth and development of each team member, the greater the success of the team.

Sometimes leaders of business and government teams seem to forget this foundation principle; they believe that once they have selected or hired a new team member, their job is finished. In reality, like parenting and coaching, the leader's real job is just beginning. There is an almost unlimited number of ways that they can provide the necessary training that leads to the growth and development of each team member. A few examples include on-the-job training by other team members, cross training (where everyone is encouraged to learn the role and responsibilities of other team members), encouraging team members to visit other organizations to learn how other teams function, refresher courses, conference participation, planned internal meetings with other areas, and other levels of leadership within the team.

Principle #2: Adaptation

Successful teams survive and grow because they are able to transform their problems into new opportunities for growth. This requires a culture in which constructive risk taking, trust, and openness to change are valued and encouraged. Being open to change encourages innovation, creativity, and preparation for future challenges.

I have experienced many changes in my life. Change is inevitable; it is a constant and necessary part of human existence. Change can be seen as an opportunity—a challenge to learn, to grow, and to improve—or it can be seen as a threat and a cause for fear. When change is embraced, it leads to growth; when change is resisted, it leads to stagnation. Things that are stagnant decay and die. Believing this, it seems obvious that everyone would welcome and embrace change. However, I believe that change is resisted by most people, even good change. Take a minute to think about some of your reactions to change. Do you ever resist change? Be honest with yourself; keep your mind open to the possibility that you may be resistant to change. Before you answer this question, I have another one to ask you: What do we really know about change? When you look closely at change, you realize that it is nothing more than a transition period, the time that exists between where you have been and where you are going.

This transition is neither positive nor negative, and what may appear to be a disaster today may someday be viewed as a blessing.

I remember when the University of Oregon dropped men's gymnastics while I was the coach. We had enjoyed years of success. Coaching gymnastics was my life, my job, my passion, and my dream, and it was suddenly gone. I really resisted that change. In fact, it took me a number of years to fully acknowledge that it had really happened. It seemed unfair and unjustified to me at that time. Today, I recognize that this change gave me the opportunity to grow, to learn, to expand, and to broaden myself personally. Today, I do many things that I would

55

never have been able to do if I had remained a university gymnastics coach. The change that appeared to be a disaster, that I fiercely resisted, ended up being a really positive development in my life.

Take a few minutes and reflect on your life. Can you find an example of change in your life that you resisted, feared, and fought against, only to find out later that it was a good change and beneficial or necessary for your growth and maybe even your survival?

Change is upsetting to the degree that we are emotionally attached to the old ways of doing things. The longer something has remained the same, the greater the attachment to it. The more we are attached to what we are doing, the greater the upset when change does occur. Effective leaders recognize and understand this resistance to change as normal in all people, and they use their understanding as a tool to direct their decisions and actions. (Remember, even good change will be resisted by many team members.)

We are always experiencing change in our lives. You and your work team are in a constant state of transition. You and your family are in constant transition. You and I are in transition together on our journey to getting Even Better. During our journey, many of the things that I will share with you may require a change in your thinking. If you find yourself resisting some of these ideas, it's okay, it's normal; simply become aware of your resistance and continue with an open mind.

Since change is a part of our day-to-day reality, it is useful to recognize some of the more interesting characteristics that accompany all types of change. Select one of your teams and see if you can identify some of these signs of change:

- Low stability
- High emotional stress
- High and often undirected energy
- A focus on control (rather than teamwork)
- Past patterns of behavior becoming highly valued
- An increase in conflict

By acknowledging these signs, you can begin to understand that certain behaviors in yourself and others are normal and predictable when in transition.

If you see any of these signs in yourself, in your work team, or within your family, don't interpret them as being bad or good, just be aware that they are normal responses to the change that you are experiencing. One of the most difficult transitions for many of us is moving from one home to another. Even if the new home is a welcome change, the transition between the old home and the new one is almost always stressful and can create all of the undesirable characteristics of change. We have all heard stories about families that have almost reached a Level 1 disagreement while moving. Don't blame yourself or others for these normal reactions; understand them and realize that they will pass when the transition period ends.

Change is always easier when people are open and willing to listen to one another, where trust and open communication occur, where conflicts and disagreements are quickly resolved, and where looking forward to the future is encouraged and discussed.

John Wooden (perhaps the greatest collegiate basketball coach in the sport's history) stated that one of the most important reasons his teams stayed on top and continued winning for so many years was their willingness to be open to the possibility that there might be Even Better ways to do things. Coach Wooden not only acknowledged this, he did something about it. He constantly had his teams scouted, asking other players, coaches, officials, friends, and spectators what they saw and what they thought could make his teams Even Better. He attributed much of his success as a coach to his willingness to ask for help from others and listen to their ideas and suggestions. Considering that there may be an Even Better way to do things, and being willing to make changes, is a common characteristic among all successful leaders.

Being open to change encourages creativity, enables innovation, and prepares you for imminent future changes.

Coaching Hint

Believe it or not, the greatest enemy of success and winning is success and winning. Once we have experienced success, we want to repeat it, and we try to accomplish it by using the same strategies and techniques that we believe created the initial success. We are frequently afraid to change anything because the thing that we change might be the very thing that created the success. We are all reluctant to change because of our fear of the unknown and our fear of failure.

Principle #3: Alignment

Successful teams achieve their goals and accomplish their desired results when the values, mission, and actions of all team members are in alignment. When all of the members of a team are in alignment, a clear game plan can be developed to provide the winning direction for all team members.

When I think of the word "alignment," I think of my car; when my car is out of alignment, I always know it. I can feel it, I can see it, and I know that if I don't fix it very soon, it will only get worse. Teams that are out of alignment have similar characteristics: you can feel it, you can see it, and you know that something is wrong. You may not immediately know what or why, but you sense that if you don't fix it very soon, it will get worse.

In sports, sometimes a team is out of alignment. A university coach was recruiting an athlete. During the recruiting process, the coach shared his dream for his team with the prospective athlete. He said, "Come to my university; we will teach you the athletic skills that are necessary for you and our team to win, and we will also work with you in the pursuit of your academic education and your degree." After some thought and comparison to other universities and other coaches, the athlete said, "Great! That is my dream too: to become a great athlete on a great team and get my degree at a university that is committed to my personal goals and my well-being. I want to accomplish all of my dreams with a coach who really cares about me as a person and who cares about more than just winning on Saturday."

The athlete enrolled at the university and started attending classes; practice began, and things were going well for everyone. The athlete was rapidly learning the skills of the sport and doing well in the classroom. As he moved into his second year, his studies became more demanding, as did the team practices and the competition. Finally, tired and frustrated, the athlete told the coach that practice and his studies were taking too much time; he could no longer do both very well. The coach's response: consider changing to a less-demanding major or reduce the academic load and focus more on the team. The coach also suggested that he could always graduate after his eligibility as an athlete was completed. This was the first test of alignment!

The athlete soon realized that his dream and the coach's dream were no longer in alignment. What was said during the recruiting process and what the coach said later did not match. This lack of consistency, and the resulting lack of alignment, led to disagreement, followed by blame, anger, and resentment; ultimately, it caused the athlete to leave the team. Unfortunately, this sequence of events is not only common among athletic teams, it is also common in business, government, and even family teams.

The hiring process in the world of business can be very similar to the recruitment of athletes. A representative of the business team tells the prospective employee about the company's commitment to provide quality products and good service to all of their customers. Soon after the prospective employee agrees to become a member of the team, she learns that the company's leaders actually allow (and even encourage) shortcuts in production that lead to poor quality. She also discovers that the leaders do not adequately train team members so they have the skills required to provide quality service for their customers.

In government, leaders are frequently selected by vote. Soliciting votes is similar to recruiting athletes and hiring employees in business. The process traditionally starts with the candidates talking about what they believe in, what they stand for, what they have already accomplished, and what they will do when elected. However, once they are elected, many of their actions are not in alignment with what they have promised.

Family teams can also be out of alignment. Some parents talk to their children about the values of being honest and fair in all of their activities. However, the parents' actions are out of alignment with their stated values when they cheat on taxes, exceed speed limits in their cars, and ask their children to "say that we are not here right now" when an unwanted caller asks for them on the phone.

Another common example of misalignment: leaders of business and government teams talk about how important it is to serve their customers and the people they represent with respect and compassion. At the same time, they yell at their employees, degrade them, and embarrass them by pointing out their mistakes as failures.

What is as equally important as recognizing a team that is out of alignment is having the tools to regain team alignment.

Team alignment must start with the team leader. It starts when the team leaders declare the desired results for their team, when they share their personal dreams and expectations for their team. This initial declaration provides a road map that every team member can follow. It also provides the foundation for the team leader to constantly reinforce and redefine these desired results, with details about how to accomplish them.

Many years ago, while I was coaching gymnastics at the University of Oregon, I saw this process displayed by our football coach. Every Monday at noon, there was a booster group meeting at a downtown hotel for fans; coaches from different sports attended as well. While waiting for my turn to speak, I listened to our football coach summarize the game from the previous weekend. After his brief summary, he began talking about the next game, which was with Stanford. He told everyone that Stanford had an outstanding team and an outstanding quarterback.

He continued by talking more about this outstanding quarterback and made it very clear to everyone in attendance (which included a couple of his players, a few members of his coaching staff, members of the media, as well as many boosters) that to beat Stanford, Oregon must shut down their outstanding quarterback. I felt that his comments were very obvious and repetitious.

After he finished, I made my presentation and returned to the university to prepare for my team's practice. Later in the week, I became aware of how effective the football coach's presentation (that I thought was unnecessary) actually was. During his practices, he repeated the same comment, almost word for word, to all of his team members: "To beat Stanford, we must shut down their quarterback."

On Monday evening, I was reading the local newspaper, and the sports page repeated the comment made by the football coach at the booster club meeting: "To beat Stanford, we must shut down their quarterback." On Tuesday, a few of the assistant coaches were interviewed by the media; their comments were: "To beat Stanford, we must shut down their quarterback." These interviews were printed in that evening's paper and repeated on the local radio and television stations. On Wednesday, a few of the players were interviewed: when they were asked how they were going to beat Stanford, they answered, "To beat Stanford, we must shut down their quarterback." And these interviews again appeared in the paper and on the radio and television.

Being a fan and booster of Oregon sports, I went to the game that Saturday. Before the game started, while visiting with friends at a tailgate party, the topic of conversation was how Oregon could beat Stanford. The answer? Right! "To beat Stanford, we must shut down their quarterback." Wow! I finally got it.

The coach's remarks at the booster meeting on Monday resulted in all of the assistant coaches, all of the players, and all of the boosters being in alignment about how to accomplish their dream. I also learned from this experience that people will parrot what leaders say. Leaders must be very careful to only talk about what they want repeated. The more often something is repeated (helpful or harmful), the more the idea will be accepted and supported. How important is having everyone on a team aligned for a common purpose? This is another question for you to answer for yourself. My answer became very clear: if I want support from my team members, I must continually talk about my dream and my desired results and how I believe they can be accomplished.

By the way, Oregon won that game, beating a heavily favored Stanford team by shutting down their quarterback.

Another example came many years later, while I was working as a team-building consultant with the US Postal Service in Oregon.

The postmaster for many small local post offices in the southern part of Oregon shared with me how she had applied the principle of alignment.

Her method was very simple: she started every meeting and every conversation, in and out of the postal system, by sharing her dream for the postal system, followed with how she felt it could be accomplished. She also presented a clear road map for their action steps to make the dream a reality. The results: better employee and customer understanding of what she wanted and how it could be accomplished.

Her efforts and her results were soon recognized and acknowledged at a national level, and she moved on to become the postmaster general in Boston, one of the largest postal systems in the country.

I encourage you to spend a little time thinking about your teams; are they in alignment? Do all of the members "walk the talk"? Have you found the dream, articulated it frequently, and gotten your team members to agree to it? Are they still aligned with it?

Principle #4: Contribution

Successful teams are developed and maintained by understanding and embracing the basic need for all people to feel that what they do is valued. Winning teams are characterized by every individual having clarity of their roles and responsibilities, allowing them to understand the necessity and value of their personal contributions.

The principle of contribution addresses a basic human need. How important is it to fully understand this statement?

"Contribution is a basic human need."

When one of our basic human needs is not met, the dying process begins. Obvious examples of human needs include air, water, and food. I believe the drive to contribute, to make a difference in this world, to make a difference in someone's life, is much more than just a desire: it is also a basic human need. We all want to feel that what we do is of value, to our families, to our jobs, and to our communities.

This basic need to contribute can be observed in children at a very young age. Young children want to help their parents do everything: cook meals, wash dishes, and clean the house (among other things).

When they come home from kindergarten, they often tell their parents why everyone should stop smoking or lose weight. When they are teenagers, they certainly don't hesitate to give advice about how they should be raised. These are just a few examples of efforts by children to contribute to their families and to feel of value (even though they do not have a conscious awareness of this human need). Keep your listening open!

Even though we all need to contribute, I also believe that we all have a built-in resistance to accepting and acknowledging others for their efforts to contribute. Wow! If this is true, we have a world full of people who want to contribute to others (their teams, their families, their loved ones) but instinctively resist receiving contributions themselves. Keep your listening open! Understanding and accepting this concept will be of great value to you as a team leader and as a team member. Let's explore this idea together. Then you can make your own decision.

When my son was about three years old, he always wanted to contribute by "helping" his mom and me do things. One day, I was outside painting the house; he came running up and asked, "Can I paint too, Daddy?"

I immediately envisioned paint all over him, the bushes, the lawn, and me. So I replied, "Not now, Billy. Why don't you run over to your friend's house and play with him for a while?"

My suggestion for him to play with his friend was my effort to avoid the anticipated mess that he would create. Children's enthusiastic efforts to contribute frequently end up being more work for us than had we just done it ourselves. I now understand that helpful children are really just trying to fulfill their basic need to contribute to their parents and to their family team. Our resistance does not make us bad parents; we are simply reacting in a way that is normal and natural. Ironically, once our children mature to an age when they are physically and mentally capable of making more meaningful contributions around the house, they often don't want to help anymore.

I remember one other painful example of me resisting a contribution that involved one of my daughters. It was her first year in college, and she was really strapped for money. For Christmas, she bought me a gift that clearly cost more than her restricted budget would allow. Upon receiving this gift, I immediately said that she shouldn't have spent her money on me and that she should have saved it for school. I continued by telling her all of the reasons why she shouldn't have bought me such an expensive gift, but in doing so, I was also taking away the real meaning of the gift: her effort to contribute to me.

Was my reaction that of an uncaring father? I don't think so. My reaction was human. I believed that I had a good reason for reacting the way that I did. However, regardless of my reason, the result was I took away some of her enjoyment to fulfill her basic human need to contribute. I could have simply accepted her gift and said, "Thank you. I enjoy your gift, I appreciate it, I value it, and I love you."

Let's look at this basic need concept from a historical perspective. Before the 1800s, our country was mostly rural, and many families lived on farms and were responsible for providing the majority of their own food. Families were larger then for a reason: every member had a vital role to play for the family to survive. There were chores to be done: fences to be mended, animals to care for, cows to be milked, eggs to be gathered, and laundry to be washed. All meaningful, valued, and necessary contributions to the family team. Today, there are relatively few families that live on farms, fewer yet that grow all of their own food and depend on each other for survival.

Tell me, what is the essential role that children play in families today? The need to contribute was necessary those many years ago, and it is equally necessary now. Today in most families, children do not have well designed roles or responsibilities that fulfill their basic need to contribute, and even when they try to contribute, their efforts are frequently resisted.

What do you think happens to children when their basic needs to contribute are resisted again and again? What do you suppose happens to people of any age who try and try and try to contribute to their teams, to their families and loved ones, only to have their efforts resisted, not recognized, or not acknowledged? We know one answer: many just quit trying.

Without essential valued responsibilities to perform within the family team, many teenagers seek other areas or teams where they can contribute and feel valued. Sometimes they find a club at school or get a job; some find their answers in sports or in church. Other opportunities to contribute to teams may be found in Boy Scouts or Girl Scouts. Some young people turn to gangs to feel wanted and necessary; youth gangs often fill the void in their family team by providing opportunities for each member to contribute and to feel valued (unfortunately, some of their contributions are outside the law).

Remember when your parents gave you advice as a teenager? How did you respond? With resistance? If you have children, you know that many times when you try to give them good advice, they do not listen. Not listening is another form of resistance. Have you noticed how some bosses respond to the advice of new employees? Or how some leaders respond to advice from anyone?

Sometimes even our best intentions as parents to create valued roles and responsibilities for our children that make them feel valued as family team members backfire.

Many years ago, when my son Billy was about fourteen years old, I remember asking him to pick up a gallon of milk after school for dinner that night. When I returned from work that evening, dinner was almost ready. I asked about the milk and learned that he had failed to get it. I was tired and annoyed, and like the other family members, I wanted milk for dinner. So after giving Billy a dirty look and adding a few choice words about responsibility, I got back into the car, drove to the store, and picked up the milk. When I arrived back home, dinner was being served. Rather than creating a big scene, I simply sat the milk on the counter, gave him another glaring look, and seated myself for dinner, grumbling inside about his lack of self-discipline. The story is not too far removed from what occurs in millions of families daily. Looking back now, I realize that I was teaching him a lesson that I had not intended: I was teaching him that if I asked him to do something and he didn't do it, I would do it for him. I demonstrated to him that he was not essential for the family team to exist; in this case, he was not even essential to get the milk on the table. I had inadvertently taught him that if he didn't do his job, if he didn't fulfill his family obligation, then I would. Take a few minutes to think about one of your teams; have you ever had your efforts to contribute resisted? Now, think about the times that you have resisted efforts by others to contribute to you. I can almost hear you say, "When I resisted the efforts of others to contribute to me, it was for a good reason; they didn't know what they were talking about or they just didn't understand the whole story." (Remember my good reasons for resisting my daughter's Christmas gift?) We can always find a good reason for our resistance; however, regardless what the reason is, it is still resistance. When efforts to contribute are resisted, there are natural ramifications: disappointment, hurt feelings, separation, and sometimes even anger and resignation.

Had that same scene happened in a rural family in the 1800s, the scenario would have been quite different. If it was my son's job to put milk on the table, and he had failed to milk the cows, what would have happened? No milk for dinner. That lesson would have clearly taught him that if he didn't do what he was responsible for, we as a family team would suffer. The deeper lesson that each of us would have learned was that he was a necessary, essential, contributing member of our family team.

Have you ever been in such a hurry that you've done someone else's work for him or her? Of course; we all have! We frequently do this to help a team member or to speed up a project. Sometimes we do it to demonstrate our annoyance or to make a person feel bad for not caring enough to get the job done correctly. Sometimes we just want to show the person how easy it is for us to do it. There are many legitimate reasons to do someone else's work; however, when you do so, you are taking away his or her chance to contribute to the team and to feel valued.

As I thought about this whole idea of contribution, I wanted to know more about how highly successful leaders effectively utilized it. We asked Lute Olson, the legendary basketball coach at the University of Arizona, to share his thoughts about the importance of contribution; specifically, we asked, "What do you do with the substitutes at the end of your bench?" (If you are not a basketball fan, the end of the bench is where you find the players that usually don't play very much.) We wanted to find out how he was able to make everyone feel that they were contributing, necessary, and valued as members of the team.

He told us how he used the reserve players on his team during a game, and how he made them a valuable, necessary component for winning the game. He paired each of his reserve players with a starting player. During the game, the reserve player on the bench watched his assigned partner on the floor to assess how he was guarded, how he was covering his opponent, and so on. When a timeout was called, the player on the floor went directly to the reserve player to ask how he might be even more productive. From there, all of the players went to the team huddle with the coaches. The players on the floor would get new information from not only the coaches, but from their partners on the bench. If the player on the floor was more productive as a result of the reserve player's contribution, the team had a better chance to win the game. This gave the players on the bench a significant role in the game's outcome.

From the much needed insight gained from Lute Olson, we began to realize that this principle was being effectively implemented in many different ways, by all of the other coaches who we had interviewed (not always at their conscious level of awareness).

It is interesting to note that almost all teams—including business and family teams—have an "end of the bench." In business, the end of the bench is typically those people who are paid the least and receive the least amount of training. When I was working in different factories in the Chicago area, I frequently heard supervisors say to disgruntled workers (including me), "If you don't like it here, get out! I can get anyone off the street to do your job."

They were clearly telling us that we were not highly valued; we were on the end of their bench. In families, children are often viewed as the end of the bench; they feel like their contributions to the family team are not acknowledged, valued, or necessary for the family to succeed.

When I worked with parents and business and government leaders, I found that successful leaders refused to treat any of their team members as being on the end of the bench. Everyone on their teams (without exception) was absolutely essential for the team to succeed. How did they do it? Good question. Everyone has a specific role and certain responsibilities that they are expected to perform. Even the disgruntled factory workers and the youngest child in the family are required to make valued contributions to their teams.

Is this just lip service? I don't think so. Successful leaders create environments in which everyone feels essential to the team. All team members know their role; they know exactly what they must do to be a contributing, valued member of the team. It is also important that everyone knows the roles and responsibilities of all other team members so everyone understands each other's value to the team.

Let's do a sports "what if" example. Pretend that we are on a six-person basketball team (rather than the standard five-person team) and I am the sixth player. You are the team's point guard, which means that you set up plays for the rest of the team. As the game begins, all six of us run up and down the floor. We pass the ball back and forth. I want to contribute and help the team win, so I call for you to throw me the ball. However, there are no plays designed for me—the sixth man—so no one passes me the ball.

I run up and down the floor and become more insistent, yelling, "Throw me the ball!" Soon you and the other players get annoyed with my presence and tell me that I am just in the way. However, I continue to run up and down the floor and ask for the ball, with no success. Eventually, I start to get tired and begin to run slower and slower. The more I try to help, the more everyone resists my efforts.

Finally, I stop running back and forth and just watch you guys play. Feeling unneeded, unwanted, and of no value to the team, I begin to resent you, the coach, and the other players for not letting me be a part of the team. You see, I have not been able to satisfy my basic human need to contribute to the team. You and the rest of the team also react in a predictable way, by resisting my efforts. Sure, I know I was the sixth man, not really necessary; I know that no plays were designed for me. But no matter how you word it, everyone resisted my efforts to help, and it bothered me.

When team members feel unwanted or of little value to a team, they can react in many different ways. They can quit the team, they can remain on the team and do very little work, or they can remain on the team and create problems.

Have you ever felt like the sixth person on one of your teams, unwanted, unneeded, and unnecessary?

Coaching Hint

Every person on a team must have an essential role with responsibilities that are necessary for the team to succeed.

If there is a position on a team that is not absolutely essential, eliminate the position or create new responsibilities that are valued. When anyone, regardless of their age, does not feel valued and is not fulfilling their basic need—to contribute—the slow process of dying begins.

As I was researching and developing the Nine Principles of Winning Teams, my dad's health began to fail. We did not see one another very often during those years, as we lived about two thousand miles apart. We talked on the phone every few weeks, and as time passed, I began to notice that his speech was slower and seemed to lack enthusiasm. He talked more and more frequently about nearing the end of his road. He was eighty-two years old then, but his medical exams indicated that he was still in good health, with no apparent physical problems. Regardless of this, he seemed to be failing. I should have known there was a problem when I realized that he kept coming out of retirement, each time going back for more work. However, when he was eighty, he retired again, and it looked as if he would stay that way.

Finally, a light came on for me: Dad no longer felt that he was a valued member of a team. I began to wonder if he had resisted retirement for so long because he felt needed and valued by his work teams. In our family team, my sister and I had made our own lives; we were both independent and doing well, and Dad had provided for our mom financially. Maybe, just maybe, he no longer felt that his efforts to help us were needed, that he was no longer of any value to our family. The light got brighter: That was the problem. Dad no longer felt that he was contributing to anyone, and the result was obvious: he was dying. He was giving up. But after coming to this conclusion, I wondered what I could do about it. Based on my belief in the principle of contribution, I realized that I needed to create a situation where he could contribute and feel valued, where he was acknowledged and felt necessary.

As a parent of three children, I know that there is no better way for parents to feel valued than by helping their children. I began to think about a way for Dad to help me: what could he do to contribute to me? How could he do anything for me from two thousand miles away? I decided to create a way for him to help me with my research and writing. At first glance, it seemed straightforward and simple for me to just ask him for his help. Great idea, right? Wrong! Remember, being human, I have a natural resistance to accepting contributions from others, especially my dad.

When I was eighteen, I told him, using my best John Wayne posture, "I can stand on my own two feet. I don't need your help. I don't want your help. I can make it without you; I can do it all on my own, and I will prove it to you." I spent the next thirty years convincing Dad and myself that I could stand on my own two feet, that I could make it without him. How could I possibly ask him for help now? Do you see the dilemma? I believed that if I asked him for his help, and if he was willing to help me, together we could form a team with a new task, and perhaps he would regain his spark for life.

As simple as that decision may seem now, it was not easy then. Many legitimate reasons seemed to stop me from going to him. I thought of many creative ways to ask for his help but still hesitated. I finally made the decision to just ask him for his help. I told him about my research and said that I was writing a book about team building. I simply asked him if he would help me write it. It was tough for me to ask him for his help, and I probably didn't do a very good job of asking. It had been thirty years since I had asked him for anything. I'm sure that he was equally surprised to get my request.

His response was not a whole lot better stated than my request. He sent me a letter. The content of the material that he mailed to me was sparse, but I immediately responded by calling him and told him that I had received his letter and really appreciated his ideas for the book. After rereading his letter, I had another stroke of genius: I should ask him about sales. He had been a salesman for a number of years. Sales are about people, right? Team building is about people, right? So I asked him for his help once again; this time I was more specific. I asked him to share some of his sales ideas with me. This seemed to raise his interest level, as this was his area of expertise.

Coaching Hint

When you are looking for a way to ask someone to contribute to you, always try to identify their area of interest or expertise and ask them a question about that (information and knowledge are forms of contribution).

The next letter I received was more detailed, more explicit, and more valuable to me. I immediately wrote back and thanked him for his letter, told him of its value to me, and asked him for more. This routine continued for the next few months. I also spoke with my mom, and she told me that he must have been feeling better because he was back to his usual grumpy self again (a sure sign of wellness in Dad!).

As time passed, the letter writing and calls became more frequent, the content of his letters was of greater value, and his level of enthusiasm was on a continuous upward path. After one and a half years and boxes of accumulated letters, I received a letter that included a newspaper clipping from a Kankakee, Illinois, newspaper. The clipping read: "Earl Ballester writes book for his son, Bill, on the West Coast." Is that great or what? In the article I also learned that Dad, without even consciously understanding the principle of contribution, had been applying it. He had asked five of his buddies to help him help me write a book. These five men, along with my dad, had been meeting every Friday for lunch for months. Their agenda was to help Earl's son, Bill, write his book. They discussed the book, each contributing in his own way, each feeling of value, each feeling that he was making a contribution to the writing of this book. These six men, all over eighty years of age, had contributed from their vast reserves of knowledge and experiences.

I was receiving far more than I had requested, not only about sales but about religion, politics, and many other topics. What was really great: their material had a significant impact on this book and on my public speaking. Dad and his five friends influenced my thinking and the methods that I used for team building and leadership training throughout the country.

The gift that I chose to give to my dad was to let him contribute to me, which in turn allowed him to once again feel valued as a father. This is a story about being allowed to contribute. Dad and each of his friends were fulfilling their basic human need; they were of value. This story is also about moving beyond the natural human tendency to resist contributions from others.

A few years later, I was in the Chicago area for a leadership training conference. Dad invited me to join his five friends for lunch at the same restaurant where they had been meeting and developing all of the material they sent me. It was great to meet them and to personally acknowledge and thank them for their contribution to me and my book. My brief remarks seemed to bring a new alertness to the group; almost as one, they asked, "Where's the book?"

Finally, after many years, here is my answer to their question: *Even Better!* is the book. My one regret is that Dad never saw this completed version. Dad passed quietly a few years later, at the age of ninety-two. We talked a lot during the month preceding his death, and even though his physical health was failing, he still had a spark; he still found enough energy to offer me his ideas on how to complete my book. He soon passed, knowing that he had helped his son. He passed, knowing that he was not only loved, but he was of value and valued.

I have told Dad's story to thousands of people throughout the world, each time watching the various responses from each audience. I have seen happy smiles, tears of joy, and also tears of sorrow. I invite you to look at your own reaction. Is there anyone, of any age, in your life who may feel that they are not valued, that they are not fulfilling their basic need to contribute to others? How about your parents? We may think that we do not want to be a burden to our parents or our loved ones; we feel that they have worked hard all their lives and deserve a rest from taking care of us and dealing with our problems. We are hesitant to intrude on their space, to ask for their help, and many times we do not let them help us when they want to. When we resist their efforts to contribute to us, we take away the one thing that every parent wants to do: in some way, in some form, contribute to their children. Give your parents, your family, your loved ones, a gift. Let them contribute to you. That may be the best gift that you have ever given to them and to yourself.

Principle #5: Responsible Freedom

Successful teams are developed in an environment in which responsibility and freedom are emphasized. The guidelines and boundaries for responsible behavior are clearly understood and agreed upon by every team member. Team members also have the freedom to act in accordance with their own personal needs, within the agreed-upon boundaries of responsibility.

This principle addresses an age-old problem that at one time or another confronts all teams. Within every team, there are always questions about what is enough, what is too little, and what is too much. These questions relate to rules, laws, required codes of conduct, and team boundaries. Too many laws and too many rules stifle freedom, creativity, and growth. Too few laws, rules, and boundaries lead to chaos, destructive conflict, and team failure. Leaders of successful teams are willing to constantly review all rules and policies to maintain an effective balance for everyone. The implementation of responsible freedom can create potential problems. In some families, there are two entirely different beliefs regarding the application of this principle with children; some fathers and mothers cannot agree on what is too much and what is not enough. One parent may want more rules and guidelines for their children, while the other believes that fewer rules are better for the child's development. It becomes even more complex when we realize that each child grows and matures at a different rate; rules for one child may not be appropriate for another child. Rules for a three-year-old child and a ten-year-old child are also different. Rules and responsibilities will constantly change as children grow older. There will always be new challenges that confront the child as well as the parent, such as driving the family car, educational choices, drinking alcohol, using drugs, making decisions about sexual involvement—and each of these examples requires different rules and different levels of responsibility.

How many rules are enough? This question is one that every leader must continually address to create and maintain highly successful teams. The goal of every team is to create boundaries of responsibility, through rules and laws that protect the continuation and prosperity of the team while protecting the rights of each individual team member.

When the responsible freedom principle is successfully implemented, rules and laws are fair, understood, and agreed upon by all team members. Every team member is given the freedom to grow and to make independent decisions while staying within the accepted boundaries of responsibility established by the team.

In sports, the guidelines for responsible behavior are clear, precise, written, spoken, taught, and understood; they must be followed by all teams and all team members. In sports, the rules don't change in the middle of the game. In sports, there are clear, understood, and immediate penalties for breaking the rules or exceeding boundaries, and penalties are directly proportionate to the rule that is broken. Can this be said for all teams? Are rules clear, fair, agreed upon? Are penalties for breaking the rules administered consistently for everyone? Are the penalties proportionate to the rule broken? If your answer is no, you have identified a problem that needs to be solved. Part 4 of this book discusses the ABCDE of solving problems, which will guide you through the process.

Sports teams also have rules of conduct that govern team members when they are away from the playing field. One such example is a players' curfew. A very successful basketball coach from the eastern part of the country told me the following story: Each year, before the first away game, he held a team meeting, and a discussion took place with all team members and coaches involved. They decided that to do their best every game, each player must be as physically ready as possible. This included a good night's rest, proper meals, and a committed focus to the game. They decided that players should be in their rooms by eleven o'clock the night before a game.

Once the curfew rule was established and agreed on, the conversation turned to what would happen if someone violated it. After a lengthy conversation, another agreement was reached. They all decided that anyone not in his room by eleven o'clock, regardless of the circumstances, would not be allowed to play in the game the following day.

As the weeks passed, the team enjoyed a fine season, with no curfew problems, and they were ranked among the nation's best. They traveled to Southern California for a big game that would be covered by national television. A lot was at stake. The night before the game, the team's star player did not return to his room until 11:15. This was clearly a rules infraction, clearly beyond the boundaries of the team's curfew rule. However, it was just fifteen minutes, and after all, he was the best player; there was so much at stake, and he was so strong physically; an extra fifteen minutes of rest was probably not that important for him. I'm sure many such thoughts went through the minds of all the coaches and players.

The next morning, the coach called a team meeting and reviewed the situation. He asked the players what they thought should be done. All team members, even the one who broke the curfew, agreed that there was a clear rule and a clear penalty for violating the rule; all agreed that he should not play. Everyone agreed that their integrity was more important than one game; when a team has rules, everyone must follow them. The star player did not play.

Know what? They won the game anyway.

There are many other rules and boundaries in sports, and not all of them are determined by discussion or consensus. In a football game, most teams huddle before almost every play. Eleven guys crowd together on the field and decide what they will do for the next play. They only have a limited amount of time to make their decision and execute the play. This decision is not made democratically; a single person (traditionally, the coach from the sidelines or the quarterback in the huddle) makes the decision. It works because everyone understands that this method of making decisions is necessary to quickly prepare for the next play. This unilateral decision-making process works because the coaches and players have talked about it long before game time; every player understands why it is necessary. Athletes understand that if they want to be members of the team, they must accept the decision and give their best effort to execute whatever play is called without discussion.

These examples make it clear that effective leadership requires different decision-making policies, determined by the circumstances. Regardless of how a decision is made, all successful teams and each team member must accept, support, and adhere to it. Successful leaders also encourage team members to ask questions about their decisions, rules, boundaries, and penalties.

When I was coaching, I had a rule that some other coaches felt was unfair and unreasonable. Perhaps, on the surface, it was. But this rule and my expectations were made very clear, and agreed on, before the athletes ever came to Oregon. The results of having this rule had a profound effect on the lives of each member of our team, personally and athletically.

The rule was very simple and straightforward. Practice started at 2:45 each weekday—2:45 on the clock in the practice gym. Every gymnast was to be seated on the mat in front of the chalkboard when the second hand reached the twelve at 2:45. There was no room for variable interpretation in that rule. You were either seated on the mat in front of the chalkboard at 2:45 or you were not. That was the rule. Anyone not seated in front of the chalkboard at 2:45 was required to run a mile for every minute that he was late. Period! (I had a fifteen-mile limit.) You may wonder why I made such a big deal over this one little rule. Well, this one rule set the tone for how our team functioned. It was a measurement of each member's commitment to the team and to the program.

Let's look at the results of this rule. Almost no one was ever late to practice (we usually went through an entire year without even one person breaking the 2:45 rule). Each gymnast simply planned to be at practice at 2:30 to allow for emergencies. Arriving fifteen minutes early allowed the athletes to visit, tell stories, stretch, relax, and prepare for practice. It also relieved them of any stress to get to practice at 2:45. Why was this rule so important? I'll name a few reasons, and you can probably think of a few of your own:

- We had agreed to be to practice on time.
- We didn't have to worry where our teammates were, or if they were okay or maybe had an accident.
- We didn't penalize those who came on time by making them wait to start practice for those who were late.
- We could, at exactly 2:45, begin our practice as a team, with our focus on the day's work and the team, not on individuals who weren't there.

There was another important reason: I didn't have to evaluate someone's reason for being late. There are lots of legitimate reasons for coming to practice late. But regardless of the reason, when someone is late to practice, it is always a distraction.

Years later, I worked with a major lumber company that chose to decide that there were some "good reasons" to be late for work.

(I'm sure that you already know how I reacted to this situation.) Each day, supervisors were forced to monitor employees' arrival time. When employees showed up late for work, there were frequent arguments and lengthy discussions as to why they were late and if their reasons for being late were justified (or even true). Whatever excuse the company allowed became the excuse everyone used. When people agree to come to work at a specific time and they don't keep those agreements, even for "good" reasons, separation between team members occurs. This separation increases because of subjective evaluation by supervisors; accepting some excuses while rejecting others usually results in anger, blame, and even resentment.

The company soon learned that if they allowed team members to be late to work three times before they were penalized, many would automatically use all of their "no penalty" days. The same was true for sick days. If team members were given seven days a year for sickness, almost all of them took the seven days off. The company decided, after two years of struggling to find a better answer to their "on time" problem, to make being on time each day a condition of continued employment. Sound similar to the 2:45 rule?

Have you ever worked in this type of environment? If so, then you'll understand what I am referring to. One thing we all learned: when someone isn't at work, that person is not a contributing, productive member of the team.

Members of many teams do not know their team's rules or boundaries or the ramifications for breaking them. When rules are not known or understood, team members may inaccurately believe that their boundaries are very restricted and become afraid to make decisions independently, for fear they might break the rules and suffer the consequences.

I once asked the members of a business team what it would take for them to be fired from their jobs. Their answers were wide ranging: being loud or rude with customers, making a mistake at their workstation, getting in an argument with a boss, coming late to work three times, taking too long for a rest break, and saying the wrong thing to someone at the wrong time. I then asked their boss the same question: what would a team member have to do to get fired? After a few minutes of thought, he gave me a short and simple answer: criminal conduct.

Engaging in criminal conduct was the boss's sole grounds for firing an employee.

I told him some of the answers given by his team members, and he was genuinely shocked to learn that they didn't know the rules and boundaries for their team. He then began to understand why so many of his team members seemed unwilling to make independent decisions, and why everyone always came to him for answers to some very routine situations.

Together, the boss and I learned a few things that day: (1) the leader of a team must take time to create rules and boundaries and *inform* all team members what they are and the penalties for not complying, (2) team members must learn the rules and the boundaries so they can function independently, with freedom to make choices and decisions within those rules and boundaries, and (3) all teams must continually evaluate and question rules and boundaries with the intention of creating more independent freedom.

In families, young children have a very limiting set of boundaries: there are rules about where they can play (stay out of the street), how they can play (don't throw rocks at your friends or their homes), and who they can play with (choose your friends wisely). As they grow older, they continually push these boundaries; slowly their boundaries expand, their responsibilities increase, and their level of freedom to make independent decisions grows. The goal, as parents, is to shepherd children through these restrictive, necessary boundaries while giving them the freedom to enlarge their options until the day arrives when they are completely independent.

I have one final story about rules. This rule can apply to all teams, but I think that it is even more important in sports and in family teams. When I was a high school coach, I had a team rule prohibiting athletes from smoking cigarettes. There was no gray area, and the choice was entirely up to the athlete. During this same time, there was a highly successful high school coach in Chicago; I respected him greatly, because of his unparalleled success with his teams. He had competed in the Olympics years before and was considered by many to be one of the finest gymnastics coaches in the world. For our story, I will call him Bill.

Bill and I had many discussions about gymnastic techniques, about dealing with young men, and about various rules and regulations for our teams. He did not have a rule about smoking cigarettes, and this just didn't seem right to me. One day, we were having an intense conversation about our different beliefs about smoking; I have never forgotten this conversation. First, he asked me, "Do you believe that gymnastics has educational value for those who participate?" Of course, I said yes. Then he asked, "Do you believe that there is value for your gymnasts to be in the gym training with you and your team?" After I answered yes again, he asked, "Do you feel that smoking cigarettes is harmful to a person's health? Do you feel that by smoking, a gymnast is not living up to your expectations?" Again I responded yes to both questions.

He concluded by paraphrasing what I had said: gymnastics is good and smoking is bad for young people. I confirmed his summary. He then asked what would happen if one of my gymnasts was caught smoking? I told him that they all knew the rules and the penalties for breaking them: the athlete would be dropped from our team.

He continued by once again restating my words and actions: so gymnastics is good and smoking is bad, and athletes who break your rules are eliminated from the team. His next statement has stayed with me through these many years and has influenced many of my decisions as a team leader. He concluded, "So as a result of your rules and actions, you have removed the good from the young man (gymnastics) and you have left him with the bad (cigarettes). Is this correct?"

Wow! Do I need to say more? If we as parents, as coaches, as team leaders are committed to help each person on our teams to grow, to mature, and to learn, we must take a long, hard look at our rules, regulations, and penalties to make sure that they are consistent with our main purpose, which is to help others become Even Better.

Now it's your turn to do a little work. Select a team that you lead and answer the following questions:

- Does this team have rules?
- Are there ramifications for breaking the rules?
- Does this team have boundaries?
- How were the boundaries determined?
- Are there ramifications for exceeding the boundaries?

- Are there ongoing opportunities to discuss the reasons and logic behind the boundaries, the rules, and the penalties?
- Does everyone on the team have the same level of understanding about the rules and boundaries?
- What boundaries are helpful to the team?
- What boundaries might be detrimental to the team?
- What would it take to get a team member dismissed?

If you are not sure what your team members know, find out. Ask them. Bring your team together and have a conversation about the existing rules and boundaries. If necessary, create new ones that are precise, decisive, and understood by everyone. Finally, make sure that everyone agrees to live within these boundaries. Next, create clear, understood, and agreed-upon ramifications for breaking the rules. Finally, let your team go and give them the freedom to function, to question the boundaries, and to push against them.

Coaching Hint

Great leaders create environments where growth is encouraged and acknowledged, where rules and ramifications for breaking rules are clear, understood, acknowledged, and continually questioned by everyone. Team growth is the result of questioning what we accept as correct and constantly reaching for new, higher levels of freedom.

Principle #6: Integrity

Successful teams are developed and maintained in an environment where everyone does what they say they will do. By demonstrating their personal integrity, effective leaders receive the highest levels of integrity, commitment, and loyalty in return.

People often think of integrity in terms of being honest, moral, or righteous in the religious sense. This is not the meaning that I will share with you here. It is a way of being, rather than a thing to do. Integrity, as defined by *Webster's*, is a "state of being whole or entire." Integrity describes the condition of a structure, an environment, or an individual as being in a sound, unimpaired condition.

During the time when Larry and I were trying to develop a clear, easily defined, and easily understood way to state the principle of integrity, I was working as a leadership consultant in a lumber mill that specialized in laminated beams that support all types of roofs, including homes, businesses, and large gymnasiums. Each beam is composed of numerous 2x4s, 2x6s, or 2x8s of various lengths. They are dried, glued, and then pressed together to form large laminated beams. One day, while moving through the plant talking with workers, I noticed the word "integrity" was stamped on a beam. I asked one of the workers what this meant. He explained that each finished beam was stamped with "integrity" to indicate its ability to perform a specific function without failure. The beams were subjected to rigorous specification tests before they were stamped and declared to have integrity without structural flaws.

This analogy best describes all teams and individuals who have integrity. They are whole, complete, and do what they say they will do. Integrity is demonstrated by team members making a declaration of what they believe in and what they stand for, and then going about doing it: "walking the talk." Just as the laminated beam says, "I'm this long, I'm this wide, I'm this strong, I will support this much weight, and I will support the roof of your building." The beam doesn't just say it, it does it. The beam would not have integrity if it did not perform to those stamped specifications by sagging or breaking. People who do not do what they say they will do also lack integrity.

We all find ourselves out of integrity on occasion, and I believe we know when we are. When we do what we know is out of integrity or against the rules, or when we do something that we know is not in another person's best interest, or when we don't do what we have said we will do, we know it; we feel it and we suffer the natural ramifications. Lack of integrity creates uneasiness, concern, and anticipation of loss or failure; it creates a feeling of unwholesomeness in ourselves and in others. Lack of integrity on a team is like a basic flaw that inevitably creates failure. A lack of integrity by a leader or team member is soon discovered by other team members; it causes tremendous amounts of energy to be directed toward judgment, justification, arguments, and disagreements, all of which distract from the focus of the team. Eventually, we all become aware of the natural ramifications for being out of integrity.

In a perfect world, we would all have integrity; we would all do exactly what we say we will do, how and when we say we will do it, just as the laminated beam states. However, this is not a perfect world; humans are not perfect.

Coaching Hint

When you share your dream and goals with your team, include your commitment to integrity. Make a declaration: "This team is going to be whole. We are who we say we are, and we will do what we say we will do. We have integrity."

Principle #7: Positive Learning Cycle

Effective leaders use a method of teaching in which setbacks and breakdowns are regarded as opportunities for learning rather than failures.

Earlier, I asked you, "Do you like to fail?" I expect that you still have the same answer. No one likes to fail. No one likes to make mistakes that negatively affect their work teams or their families. Even the word "failure" creates an uncomfortable feeling in me. Yet, looking back on my life, there were many occasions when things went wrong. I failed to do what I wanted to do, failed to make good decisions, failed to inform my children of my dreams and the dreams and goals for our family team. I failed to keep some of my agreements, failed academic tests, and failed to win competitions. Yes, I felt the guilt and the pain of failure. I know that I am not unique in having experienced failure. We all fail at something, in some way or another. We all fail to do something that we have wanted or were expected to do.

In sports, it's easy to see those failures: in football, it can be a player failing to catch a pass; in basketball, it can be a player failing to make a free throw; in baseball, it can be a batter striking out. In team sports, such as football, during every play, someone may fail to do his job correctly: someone misses a block or a tackle, someone doesn't throw the ball accurately, someone drops a pass. Failure is a part of sports and a part of life, and sometimes the failures that we experience are out of our control.

How can we possibly live with all of this failure? It is reported that Thomas Edison failed more than five thousand times while trying to discover the proper element to make the light bulb illuminate. When Edison was asked, "How can you stand to be such a failure?" he answered, "I have not failed, I discovered five thousand elements that didn't work, which is five thousand fewer elements that I have to try before I find the one that will work."

How's that for persistence and the unwillingness to accept failure as an option? What Edison did was to learn from his mistakes. He moved closer to his goal through a continuous process of trying and not succeeding, trying again and again and again, never giving up, and finally discovering the element that changed the world.

To learn from our mistakes and setbacks, we must first acknowledge and take responsibility for them; next, we must let go of all thoughts of failure and try again. Some people constantly dwell on their setbacks, reliving the pain and the embarrassment again and again for years. When you don't let go of the feelings of failure, you pull in, you take fewer risks, and this reduces your chances to eventually succeed. Do you know people who are constantly reliving their failures and focusing on what didn't work? Do you know people who don't even attempt to do things because of their fear of failing, or getting reprimanded or punished? This is another sameness in all human beings: the fear of failure.

What separates those who fail and yet keep trying from those who fail and stop trying? Why do some people have the courage to keep trying over and over again? Why do some teams seem to be successful at everything they attempt, while others seem to always be at the edge of failure? The good news: there is a way to create an environment in which teams and individuals can move beyond failure; winning coaches, effective business leaders, and successful parents create environments where there is no such thing as failure. The word simply does not exist! Mistakes will continue to happen; however, all mistakes are viewed as opportunities to learn, rather than failures. This is not an easy thing to do, and no team can create an environment where the feeling of failure is nonexistent.

However, it is possible to minimize the negative effects that accompany the feeling of failure. To create such an environment, leaders must first rid themselves of the outdated belief that if a mistake is made, someone must be held responsible, someone must pay for the mistake, and someone must be punished. When leaders end this type of thinking, they will find that team members will come forward and help identify their problems. The first step to solving any problem (mistakes are problems) is to become aware of it. In an environment where people are reprimanded or feel guilty, they will naturally deny or hide their mistakes. Where errors are openly acknowledged and discussed—where people are free from reprimand and free from the feeling of failure— everyone can look at the error and work together to create a system that will minimize or eliminate similar problems in the future.

Mistakes Happen! To Err Is Human!

Even in highly successful teams where there is no such thing as failure, there are setbacks. To err is human; however, there are some leaders who seem to handle the mistakes made by themselves and by their team members more effectively than others. How do they do it? Good question.

As I continued my interviews with successful leaders from business and government teams, I added this question: How do you handle the mistakes made by you or your team? One business leader I will call George was happy to share how he had handled a recent mistake. His company had just finished printing an updated employee directory. It listed all employees' names, phone numbers, their work-related positions, their responsibilities, and their job descriptions. George was just beginning to look at the new directory when the company's vice president came into his office and informed him of an error that he had just discovered right on the cover: the company's phone number was incorrect. This was definitely a mistake, and a big one.

I asked George, "What did you do? How did you react?"

He said that he told the vice president that the new directory was not acceptable and reminded him that he was responsible for its accuracy. He also pointed out that the error was going to cost the company both time and money, adding that there were no good reasons for this type of error to occur. George also told his VP that his job was not in jeopardy, but he must find and reprimand the person who actually made the error.

My initial response to his story: George's way of handling the problem seemed okay to me. How about you? If you also think his way of handling the problem was okay, then you should look at the possible ramifications for his actions.

How do you think the VP felt after this conversation with George: embarrassed, angry, and maybe even resentful? When the VP left George's office, he probably headed straight for the person who was responsible for the mistaken phone number and re-created a similar scenario to the one he had just had with George. If you were the person who had actually made the error, how would you feel? George had focused on placing blame (Who was responsible?) rather than fixing the problem. His behavior was then modeled and repeated by the VP. Now we have three people upset: George, the VP, and the worker. To make it worse, some people take their anger and resentment home to their family teams and reenact similar scenarios with their partners or children. These upsets will continue to multiply until the mistake is corrected.

A few days after my conversation with George, I told this story to Mizo, a friend of mine who had studied business leadership in Japan, Spain, and England and was about to start a new management job in California. I asked him how he thought George had reacted.

Mizo responded that if he were George, when the VP told him about the directory mistake, he would have first thanked him for discovering the error. Next, he would have asked the VP to help him create a new system that would remove any possibility of making similar errors in the future.

Would Mizo's method to solve the problem work? I believe that it would be very effective: it would eliminate the blame, the embarrassment, and the guilt that usually leads to anger and resentment. It would also have provided a good model for the VP to follow when he confronted the worker who actually made the mistake. The results would be three people focused on creating a new and better system to avoid future mistakes, without anyone holding onto thoughts of blame or failure.

Now let me ask you, which boss would you prefer to work with: George or Mizo? The answer is fairly obvious. We would all rather not experience failure and the accompanying consequences.

Once an error is made, there are two choices a leader can make: spend time placing blame and determining some type of punishment, or immediately turn the focus to correcting the error and soliciting help from others to create a new system that minimizes human errors.

When leaders view mistakes as failures, the effects ripple through the entire team; some team members may feel so bad that they quit the team. When someone quits the team, regardless of the reason, the team leader must recruit, hire, and train a new team member, who will also make mistakes. This pattern of hiring, training, and losing team members will continue until a system is developed and implemented that overrides human errors and eliminates the fear of making mistakes.

Wouldn't you like to be a team member in an environment where, when you make a mistake, you are comfortable discussing it? Wouldn't you feel better knowing that you were safe from blame and ridicule? Wouldn't you learn faster and develop Even Better skills as a team member, a team leader, a parent? Wouldn't you feel loyalty to your team, to your team leader? Wouldn't you feel good about yourself?

Teams that are successful, where each individual grows and develops personally, have the freedom to make errors and discuss their errors without the constant threat of blame. They also have the responsibility and the freedom to work together to create new, better systems that will override human errors.

Cycles for Success

Follow each of the following steps; there is no time table, there are no rules to follow, other than keep trying. You can use this model to completely eliminate failure from your way of thinking and to accomplish all of your dreams and goals.

Here are a few hints and guidelines to consider as you progress through each step toward your success:

1. See setbacks as opportunities for growth and learning.
2. Set realistic and obtainable goals.
3. Take more constructive risks.
4. Find the way back to a beginner's mind.
(Remember when you were young, not afraid to try things, not overloaded with rules or expectations, not concerned with failure? The

strength of a beginner's mind is that you have not yet learned the feeling of failure and are still willing to try and to keep trying.)

5. Celebrate small successes along the journey.

6. Allow others to contribute to you.

7. Look for the beneficial purpose of every action and result.

Become less attached to specific results and more attached to the continued movement toward your desired result.

Cycle for Failure

This model will lead to failure in your life and within all of your teams. I am sharing this model with you so that you can easily identify the differences and avoid this destructive negative cycle.

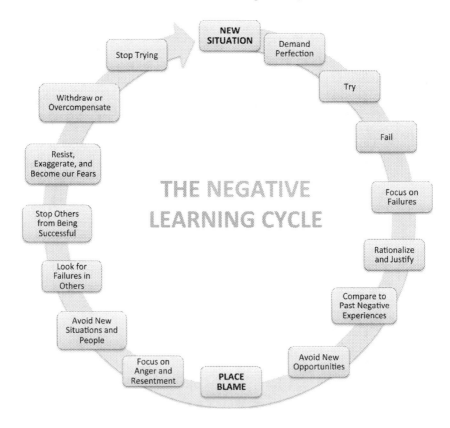

Here are a few examples of how some people continue to remain stuck in this failure model:

1. Insist on the need to be right.
2. Emphasize winning at all costs.
3. Take shortcuts.
4. Develop excuses and rationalizations for failure.
5. Compare themselves with others who have more or less than they do.
6. Avoid taking responsibility for creating their own lives.
7. Don't listen to or depend on anyone else.
8. Bury their feelings.
9. Exaggerate the importance of small details.
10. Don't take risks.

The good news: it is never too late to start using the Positive Learning Cycle for success.

Principle #8: The Balance of Extremes

Effective leaders are both highly directive and highly supportive in their relationships with their team members, and they understand the appropriate time for each style. They are able to develop a supportive environment for constructive risk taking and growth, while instilling a demand for perfection that is unyielding.

It took me a considerable amount of time to really understand and feel comfortable with this principle. There was something about the word "balance" that just didn't seem to capture the spirit of the principle. After reflection, I realized that balance was the perfect word to describe the equilibrium that exists between the two extremes in styles of leadership: directive and supportive. Let's look at these two extremes.

These styles are easier for me to explain with examples. A leader being directive would say, "Do this, and do it this particular way."

Directive leaders give team members explicit directions, telling them what to do and how to do it. A supportive leader would say, "Here's the task, here are the results that we want, now you figure out your own way to get it done, and I'll be here if you need any help."

Balancing these two extremes doesn't mean a compromise. It means that leaders must be highly directive in some situations and highly supportive in others. This can be difficult for some leaders, because it can force them to move away from their natural, comfortable style of leadership.

Another challenge for leaders is deciding when to use a directive approach and when to be more supportive. Unfortunately, there is no "one size fits all" rule. It is impossible to create a time schedule or a programmed graph describing when to be directive and when to be supportive. However, the following examples may serve as guidelines to help answer these questions for yourself and your teams.

Example 1: A New Baby Arrives

In the first few years of a baby's life, it needs a lot of direction. Everything is new to babies; they have no reference points or previous experiences that prepare them for the new things that they encounter every day. They have a lot to learn about fire, water, busy streets, big dogs, stairs, and an infinite number of other new experiences—many of which can cause injury and even death. During these early years, young children need highly directive help; they need lots of personal attention and direction. They must be taught what to do and what not to do, and when they can or cannot do it. Parents' primary job during these early years is to provide the necessary direction for them to be safe and to survive. As children grow older, they become more capable of functioning on their own with less direction. They gain more experience, until at some point they are able to survive and function with little or no direction from their parents.

This example represents the progression of children from being highly dependent to becoming independent and the corresponding progression of parents from being highly directive to supportive. Our ultimate goal as parents is to lead our children until they are capable of functioning without our direction, eventually letting go of our controlling, directive method of parenting. The transition from directive to supportive parenting is necessary for children to mature into productive, self-sufficient adults. In our society, this is usually somewhere around the ages of eighteen to twenty-one. However, some children never make it to the independent stage, while others are independent at fifteen or sixteen. Establishing the correct time to "let go" is a major challenge for almost every parent, business leader, and coach.

Example 2: In Sports

My first coaching assignment was to work with high school freshman football players. These young men were at the very beginning stages of their football experience. Many of them didn't even know how to put their uniform on correctly; many others didn't know how to use the combination locks found on their lockers. I had to teach them how to open their lockers, how to insert the protective pads into their uniforms, where to find the showers, and even where to find the practice field. Highly directive leadership was also necessary as we began to practice the skills of the game. I told them where and how to line up, and I showed them the correct way to throw and catch the ball. My method of teaching them was extremely directive, much like a parent with a new baby, because they were at the very beginning of a new experience.

The next two years, these young football players continued to learn with less and less direction from me and their other coaches. Finally, as seniors and seasoned veterans in our program, they were given the opportunity to make more independent decisions on and off the field. My role as a coach evolved from being highly directive to becoming more supportive, allowing individuals to function with more freedom to explore their own strengths and unique ways to accomplish our team goals.

Many of these young players continued their education and their football careers in college. Upon entering the university, they were once again freshmen, with a new team, a new location, a new set of coaches, a new set of rules and expectations, and again at the beginning stages of another new experience. Their college coaches also recognized that as new team members, each player needed more direction, and their method of teaching was similar to the highly directive methods that the players first experienced as freshmen in high school. As the players progressed through their years in college, the same leadership scenario from directive to supportive would occur as they progressed from being dependent to becoming independent.

A few very gifted college football players have the opportunity to continue their careers in the NFL. Guess what? Even after being highly successful college football veterans, they are once again new to their team and new to their circumstances; this time they are called rookies! These players may require a shorter period of time with direction than when they were high school or college freshmen, but they still need direction until they can successfully adapt to their new team and new environment.

Leaders must also be aware that teams are made up of people who progress toward their independence at different rates. It is rare when an entire family, business, or athletic team has everyone at the same stage at the same time. There are those who are highly dependent—children, new employees, and new players. There are those who have more experience or better skills and are capable of performing more independently with less direction and more support.

A predictable guideline that all leaders can follow: when people are new to any situation, they will require more directive supervision; as they become more experienced, more comfortable, and more skilled, they will require less direction and more support.

There are also less predictable times when more direction is necessary: when several team members are in the independent stage concurrently, each wanting to do things their own way, they will frequently compete, argue, and disagree with each other, which can quickly lead to conflict and separation. When this happens, an effective leader must step in and be more directive to keep all team members focused on what is best for the team rather than what is best for themselves. When these conditions exist, being directive means dictating levels of expectation and creating rules that are known, understood, and applied consistently to everyone.

Coaching Hint

If you are experiencing problems on one of your teams, consider the possibility that you may be too directive for certain people and certain situations and not directive enough for others. Too much direction stifles growth and creativity. Too little direction, particularly in the early stages, often leads to confusion, failure, and internal competition.

During my years of coaching at the University of Oregon, I was able to create this balance of leadership style without even consciously understanding the principle. My natural way of leading tends to move me toward the highly directive end of the scale much of the time. (Many of my gymnasts would tell you, "all of the time.") I planned and directed all team practices; gymnasts had their own workout card that I prepared for them every day. The cards told them exactly what I wanted them to work on and how many times to repeat each skill. They also had to perform each skill at a level that was acceptable to me before they could leave the gym. Does this sound like balance to you? My answer to this question is probably the same as yours: *no*. This was a highly directive method of teaching.

Thankfully, I always had great team captains and outstanding assistant coaches who provided the necessary balance for our teams. During our most productive years, most of my assistant coaches were my former gymnasts; they knew me and my leadership style very well. They accepted and supported my directive style and believed that it was necessary for the development of each gymnast and essential for our team's continued success. One of their responsibilities was to console, support, and empathize with the gymnasts; they spent time in the locker room or in their dorm rooms, assuring them that they were doing well and that I really cared for them, even though I was very demanding. They also constantly reminded the gymnasts that they were moving closer to their personal goals and the goals of the team. These team captains and assistant coaches provided the necessary support for the gymnasts, creating a balance to my highly directive leadership style.

Another part of my unconscious competency involving the principle of balance of extremes originated with zero planning on my part. We had two training areas that were physically separated; I could only be in one gym at a time. When I was in one gym, the gymnasts in the other gym had the freedom to make their own decisions, independent of my watchful eye and directive demands.

As I became aware of the need for a more supportive practice environment, I asked the team for their ideas about how this could be accomplished. Based on their input, we designed one practice each week where the gymnasts were allowed to create their own workouts. My function during those workouts was to observe, teach skills, assist, and support them in their efforts to grow independently from my direction. The result of this "free workout day" was that each gymnast experienced personal growth and higher levels of creativity; they also developed even more self-confidence.

All effective leaders have their own unique ways to reach a healthy balance between directive and supportive leadership. When leaders understand this principle and implement it effectively, a balance of leadership style is achieved and there is a natural progression for team members to move from dependence to independence and ultimately to interdependence. Interdependence is the final stage in the growth and development of team members. It is the realization that when they all work together, helping each other, everyone wins.

Your Leadership Style

What is your natural leadership style? Are you more comfortable being highly directive or more supportive?

Learn more about your leadership style by asking yourself these questions:

- ✓ When am I highly directive in my relationships with team members?
    - ○ All of the time
    - ○ Some of the time
    - ○ Never
- ✓ When am I supportive in my relationships with team members, offering little or no direction?
    - ○ All of the time

- ○ Some of the time
- ○ Never
- ✓ What stage of development are each of my team members in?
  - ○ Dependent
  - ○ Independent
  - ○ Interdependent
- ✓ Are those who I lead dependent on me to tell them what to do and how to succeed?
- ✓ Can they do a task without me telling them how, when, and where?
- ✓ Do I control the situation so much that I don't know how well they would do without my direction?

Questions and Ideas to Consider:

- ✓ Are there team members who are trying to become more independent? Are there members who seem to resist my directive methods? *If so, try being less directive and more supportive.*
- ✓ Are some team members not productive due to their lack of training and direction? *If so, be less supportive and more directive.*
- ✓ Are team members arguing, complaining, and competing with one another, causing some to feel like losers? *If so, be less supportive and more directive.*
- ✓ Do people sit around and wait for you to tell them what to do? *If so, be less directive: explain what the desired results are and let them learn from their mistakes. Support them with fewer directives.*
- ✓ Are your team members creative? Do they offer suggestions or ideas for change that make things Even Better? Are they free to make mistakes without fear of reprimand from you and other team members? *If not, become less directive and encourage them to work with you, not for you. Support their efforts.*
- ✓ Do you make most of your decisions without input from your immediate team members or from your extended team members (customers, suppliers, members from other teams that your team impacts)? *If so, ask for input from as many team members as possible.*

✓ Do team members ever get a scheduled opportunity to provide their ideas in the decision-making process? *If not, create planned meetings and ask for their input.*

Coaching Hint

When team members are asked to contribute their thoughts and ideas to the decision-making process, they will feel a degree of ownership, be more supportive, and work harder to implement your decisions.

Principle #9: Progressive Mastery

Effective leaders teach for steady improvement. Their method is to build one small success after another in a progressive manner, constantly reaching for a higher level of mastery. The continuous challenge for all leaders and all team members is to become Even Better! One step at a time.

Progressive mastery is a continuous, never ending process. It is a process of learning skills, developing understanding and confidence, and then building on those skills. It requires an environment where leaders and team members are constantly searching for and discovering Even Better ways to do things. Skills are taught and learned in incremental steps, taking each small step only after mastery of the preceding one.

Once a new level of mastery is reached, successful leaders direct their team members along a series of planned steps to further build their skills, on the shoulders of the last skill, always reaching toward even higher levels.

Effective implementation of the principle of progressive mastery requires the use of the tools and concepts taken from the other eight principles. It also requires another necessary component that is easy to recognize in sports: keeping score. In sports, keeping score is a form of objective evaluation to determine the performance levels of individuals and the combined efforts of the team.

Do you remember the story that I shared with you about America's journey to the top of the men's gymnastics world? Beginning gymnasts in Japan were required to start at a basic level #1 and were not allowed to move to level #2 until they had mastered all of the skills at level #1. Mastery of skills at each of the following levels was also required before moving on to even higher levels. By mastering all of the required skills at each level, every gymnast who advanced had the necessary foundation skills for international competition.

During this same time period, many American gymnasts seemed more interested in developing very difficult skills and spending less time developing their basic skills. American gymnasts were frequently allowed to move forward to levels beyond their mastery; by skipping these basic steps, they lacked the foundation skills that would allow them to reach a world champion level. Eventually, we began to model the Japanese training methods of progressive mastery, requiring each athlete to master the basic skills before advancing to the more difficult skills.

From Assembly Line Worker to Superior

In many US industries, highly productive assembly line workers are often promoted to a supervisory role. This is a reward for their many years of service and their mastery of the skills required for success on the assembly line. It is assumed that because the line worker is dependable, is experienced, and has a high level of skill, he or she should be able to supervise and teach others those same skills. This thinking, when combined with a lack of direction and training for his or her new position, frequently leads to the new supervisor making many mistakes and failing as a team leader. For this transition to be successful, it requires directive leadership, specific training, and time to master the new skills of the position.

This lack of progressive mastery is also very common in the world of sales, especially those salespeople who work only for commission. New salespeople are brought into a company, given very little training or direction, and immediately told to go out and generate sales. They are also given a sales quota, typically determined by past production levels of more experienced salespeople. The new salespeople go out excited, committed, motivated, and quickly realizes that they can't reach the designated sales quota because they don't have the necessary mastery of even the most basic skills required for sales. The failure rate in this type of situation is very high.

If your team members are making a lot of mistakes and experiencing frequent setbacks, they may be trying to function beyond their level of mastery of the necessary skills to successfully accomplish their tasks. Other negative signs of team members exceeding their mastery level are loss of confidence, unhealthy competition, fighting among team members, absenteeism, general lack of enthusiasm, dishonesty, failure to meet simple goals, unhappiness, and in some cases, even depression caused by the feeling of failure. When these things happen, leaders must ask themselves if they are providing the training and direction necessary for each person to be able to take small successful steps to first reach lower levels of mastery before expecting them to move to higher levels. If you were the leader of a team that was experiencing these negative signs, what would you do to correct the problem? How would you help your team members to regain their confidence and increase their levels of productivity?

If you are waiting for me to give you an answer, you will be disappointed. This time, I am going to take a more supportive position. You are ready to find those steps yourself (I will give you a hint). Step back a little and spend some time thinking about a few of the different options you have as a team leader. Try mentally reviewing some of the first eight principles; you will find answers there. You may also find an answer in the next story.

Back to the Fundamentals

When football coaches lose a game, they inevitably ask themselves why their team lost. The most common answer: "We didn't do our jobs; we didn't execute correctly; maybe we asked the players to do too many new things before they were ready." They frequently decide to go back to fundamentals, back to working on their basic skills.

For the next week, the team practices the same fundamental skills that they had worked on before losing their game.

What do you think happens when the team returns to practicing the fundamentals that they had previously mastered? Correct: they become comfortable again and more confident. By returning to the skills that they had previously mastered, they reenter their zone of mastery and regain their self-esteem and renew their hope and enthusiasm for the next game. Successful leaders of all teams teach things in a progressive order, one step at a time, being careful to not ask or require their team members to perform beyond their levels of mastery.

Finding Answers

I have used these nine principles to answer many of my life's questions. I encourage you to also use them along with the stories, the ideas, and the concepts to develop your own answers for all of your leadership questions. Your answers may differ from mine, just as others may discover their own unique ways to become Even Better. I do not know any exact formula or one surefire answer to leadership questions; however, I believe that within this model, answers can be found: ways to become an Even Better parent, an Even Better business leader, an Even Better coach, Even Better in all of your relationships.

Part Four:

How to Solve Problems

Chapter 5
Is There a Secret to Winning?

During my years as a coach and business consultant, I have been asked many times if there is a secret to winning. I know of no secret; however, I have a very simple answer: those teams that solve the most problems win. The answer is that simple: "Those who solve the most problems win."

For me, a problem is anything that stands between where I am and where I want to be; some call these things barriers, obstacles, or roadblocks. Many business consultants prefer to call them challenges rather than problems. I also know that when teams don't address their challenges, they have problems.

Usually after I have answered this first question, the next question is, How do I solve my problems? Is there an easy way? Again, my answer is, I know of no easy way to solve problems, but I do believe team problems can be solved more easily if you as a leader follow these steps:

(1) First you must become aware of the problem.
(2) Acknowledge that there is value gained by solving the problem.
(3) Acknowledge that any problem that affects the performance level of any team member is a team problem.
(4) Make a good decision to solve the problem.

(5) Take action to efficiently implement the good decision.

(6) Measure the results to determine the effectiveness of the decision made and the action taken.

Let's break each step down and take a more detailed look.

(1) How do you become aware of a problem? You create an environment for all team members where they feel safe to come forward with all of their ideas about any problems that they believe are affecting their personal performance or the performance of the team; acknowledge them for their contribution.

(2) How do you determine if there is value to gain from solving a problem? This one is easy. You ask yourself and others on the team, "If this problem is removed, would we be more productive or effective in our efforts to reach our goals?" If the answer is no, forget that problem and move on to the next one. Don't waste time trying to solve problems that, if solved, have no value to the team.

(3) How do you know if a problem of an individual team member affects all of the team? We frequently view individual team member problems as only the problem of the person who is experiencing it. Effective team leaders realize that any problem that negatively impacts the productivity of any member of the team will impact the ability of the entire team to reach its goals. Here's an example that many of us can relate to: A family member has a problem with the use of illegal drugs. Family members frequently argue about whose problem it is. Is it the individual's problem or is it the family's problem? I believe that it is the entire family's problem (grandparents, parents, brothers and sisters, even aunts and uncles), because it adversely affects everyone in the family in some way. By acknowledging it as a family problem, rather than calling it an individual's problem, the family can work together to begin finding ways to solve the problem. This family example is representative of situations found in all teams. By acknowledging all problems as team problems, everyone can focus on solving the problem, rather than focusing on who or what to blame.

(4) How do you make good decisions that lead to solving the problem? You ask for ideas and solutions from everyone who is impacted by the problem. When leaders ask for input from team members and use their information to make their decisions, members feel a sense of ownership, causing them to be more supportive and work harder to effectively implement the decision.

(5) How do you implement the good decisions once they are made? You make sure that everyone is aware of the decision. A directive leader's approach is to emphasize the value for the team once the problem is solved. Provide clarity for what is to be done, why it must be done, how it must be done, who is going to do it, and when it is going to be done. A more supportive approach would be to communicate the desired results and let the team do the rest.

(6) How do you know if your decision has solved the problem? You objectively measure the results of the actions taken by your decision, before and after implementation.

Communication: No Good News/No Bad News

While searching for more answers to the "How" questions, I interviewed a very successful businessman who had also been a top collegiate quarterback and an All-American catcher. I will call him Steve. I was anxious to interview someone who had enjoyed high levels of success as an athlete, as a coach, and finally as a business leader. He had clearly found answers to solve the many problems that he had encountered in every arena he entered.

I started our interview by asking him what he felt was his greatest challenge in all of his leadership roles. I also asked him what he believed was the most important reason for his success. "No good news, no bad news. Just news," was his immediate answer for both of my questions.

This answer meant very little to me, so I asked him, "What does that mean?"

He explained that, as a football player, a baseball catcher, a college coach, and a business leader, it was his job to make good decisions, good decisions that solved problems. Steve continued by saying the only way he could do that was to have accurate, complete information. His greatest challenge as a leader was getting the accurate information necessary to make good decisions.

Until we had our conversation, I had never thought about the differences between delivering good news and bad news. I have since learned that there is clearly a difference; few of us like to deliver bad news. Have you ever noticed how good you feel when you can go to your boss with good news: that profits are up or that the new person you hired is working out Even Better than had been expected? It sure feels good to deliver good news. It also feels good to receive good news. Right? Now, let me ask you how you feel when you have to deliver bad news: monthly projections are way down, or Dad, I just wrecked the car? How would you feel if you had to deliver the news that we must lay off 20 percent of our work force, or cut two players from our team?

The good news/bad news dichotomy can be difficult to get around. Now, compound this by a boss who gets really excited, acknowledges you, and even gives occasional bonuses when you relay good news. Or maybe your boss gets angry when you deliver bad news. The results are obvious: everyone would rather avoid delivering bad news. However, if you are the boss, the quarterback, the catcher, the coach, the parent, or the supervisor, what do you need to make a good decision? You need all of the information, not just the good information!

Steve went on to give me an example: His top employee, Bob, had discovered a production problem. One of the company's manufacturing machines wasn't functioning correctly, but Bob did not want to bother Steve with the problem (bad news). Instead of telling Steve immediately, he waited for nearly a year and a half, during which time he and other employees had to spend many extra hours keeping this very essential machine repaired and running.

Here's where it got interesting. Over the same period, Steve had been considering the purchase of a brand new computerized machine to replace the aging one. The new machine would increase production, increase profits, increase product quality, and do all of this more rapidly, more efficiently, and with less danger to workers. However, he was reluctant to replace something that was working so well. Bob didn't know that Steve was considering the new machine. Bob didn't want to trouble Steve with the bad news about the machine. He was concerned about the company not having the resources to even consider the purchase of a new machine, so he faithfully kept repairing the old one.

When Steve and Bob finally did talk, they both realized what their failure to communicate had created. After their open conversation and with their combined information, they then, and only then, could make an informed decision regarding fixing the old machine or replacing it with a new one.

After hearing this story, I understood what Steve meant by "no good news, no bad news, just news." Information was absolutely necessary for him to make good decisions to solve the problems that would lead his team to the desired results. I also had a new understanding about leadership: all leaders need accurate and timely information to make decisions to solve their problems. For leaders to get this information, people must feel free to come forward with bad news as well as good news.

We can also learn from Steve's story that as a team leader, you must constantly convey information to your team about your thoughts, ideas, and future plans.

Coaching Hint

When there is a void of information, most people fill that void with negative thoughts. It is essential for leaders to fill those voids with accurate, current information.

By now you are probably saying, "I understand how this news thing works, but how do you create an environment where errors and mistakes, setbacks, failures, roadblocks, and bad news are brought to the boss without fear of getting killed as the messenger?"

Good question. Successful team leaders model behavior that conveys the concept of "no good news, no bad news, just news" by just listening and by reducing or eliminating any emotional reaction to what they are hearing. Finally, they acknowledge and thank the person who is delivering the news, regardless of the content.

Steve reconfirmed my belief that the first step to solving all problems is to become aware of them, and this requires open, candid communication by all team members. He also helped me to realize that

Bill Ballester

lack of effective communication among team members is a common team problem, even in winning teams.

Soon after my interview with Steve, I decided to take some time away from my research and try a new adventure: off-road racing in Baja. It was during this adventure that I learned firsthand about another problem that can quickly destroy teams.

Chapter 6
Adventure in Baja

The Baja 1000 is considered by many to be the premier off-road race in the world. It is held in Baja California, Mexico: a 1,000-plus-mile peninsula that extends like a thin finger south from California's border with Mexico, with the Pacific Ocean to the west and the Sea of Cortez to the east. The Baja is known for its rugged terrain, unexplored mountains, beautiful beaches, and sparse population. A wonderful place for me to find a new adventure.

For more than a year, I dreamed of making this trip and racing a truck in the Baja 1000. I soon realized that to make my dream a reality, I would need help. I would need a team, so I began to talk with many people about my dream. I soon learned that not everyone shared my dream or even cared to hear about it. However, I continued to dream and to share it with everyone who would listen. One day, a friend mentioned that he knew a man named Tom who had often talked about wanting to see Baja and suggested that I call him. I got on the phone that same day, called Tom, and told him about my dream to race the Baja 1000. Tom wanted to hear more, and we decided to get together for lunch and talk more about this crazy dream of mine.

Soon after our meeting, Tom called me and said that he would like to be a part of my Baja team. That was the beginning of my team; now there were two of us with a similar dream. The following months, we told everyone who would listen about our dream. Ultimately, we formed a team of six committed people with a similar dream: to go to Mexico and race the Baja 1000 in a truck.

The team began to meet regularly to discuss the details of our adventure, to plan our strategy, and to determine each of our individual roles and responsibilities. There were also concerns about the cost of the trip and the time away from their businesses. By working together as a team, we were able to work out all of those details. We dealt with work schedules, financial concerns, vacations, and family obligations until we had a plan that would work for each of us. Finally we were ready, and the time was fast approaching to begin our ultimate adventure—to race the Baja 1000.

Six excited guys left Oregon in an old motor home with the race truck in tow. We were "Team Oregon," and our declaration was "Baja or Bust," which we painted on the side of the motor home.

While traveling to Mexico, we decided together as a team that our "win" would be to be safe, have fun, and finish the race. Nearing the border, we added a Spanish word and painted our "win" on the side of the race truck: "Be Safe, Have Fun, Finish = Fantastico!"

We accomplished the first step of our dream without incident: we got to Baja safely and had fun doing it, even though there were a few financial surprises at the border, like having to pay for Mexican auto insurance. With our goals clear and our wallets somewhat thinner than expected, we crossed the border into Mexico and were still safe and still having fun.

Prior to the race day, we each practiced our assigned responsibilities. Tom and I practiced driving over the rough Baja terrain, learning how the truck handled and becoming familiar with the maps that were to direct our progress. The four other team members (our pit crew) practiced coordinating their efforts for the pit stops during the race. The pit crew had to know exactly where to be for each pit stop so they would be waiting when we arrived. We would need gas about every 150 miles; during each pit stop, Tom and I could get information about our competition and make any necessary repairs on the truck. This was a huge challenge and required a committed effort and real teamwork by everyone.

We continued to prepare for race day, and our excitement was mounting along with our anxiety over the challenges ahead; we were also tired after traveling from Oregon. However, we were all committed to performing our jobs and realizing our dreams; we could rest after we finished the race.

Finally, it was race day, and everybody was ready. The pit crew headed out to their first assigned pit stop. Tom and I drove our shiny truck to the starting line, where thousands of people had gathered to see the race begin. I was behind the wheel and Tom was my co-driver; we had agreed that we would shift positions at the midpoint. Within a very short time, it was our turn to start. We quickly moved beyond the well wishing spectators, driving away from downtown Ensenada and into open country, away from the city. This was it; we were finally racing. We were finally living our dream.

About three hours into the race, while running along a dry riverbed at a good pace, Tom told me that we were rapidly approaching a right turn that would take us up a steep hill into a rocky area, and then we would pass through a small ranch. I soon spotted our turning point and executed a good turn—or so I thought. Boom—Crash—Bang—Expletives!

We hit a huge rock, which caused the truck to flip over and land on its top. There we were, somewhere in Baja Mexico, upside down in our truck, and what do you think we were doing? If you guessed crying, you are close, but not correct. We were yelling at each other! Picture a race truck with two guys in race suits and helmets, strapped in the seats, hanging upside down, waving our arms, and yelling at each other. Not a pretty picture, and it certainly wasn't fantastico.

Why were we yelling? I was yelling at Tom because he had clearly caused us to flip the truck. After all, he had failed to tell me about this big rock. For some reason, Tom was yelling at me, just because I happened to be driving the truck. We continued our yelling until, suddenly, Tom (obviously the smarter) commented that gasoline might be running onto the hot engine and could cause a fire. Following that realization, and the fear that we could die if the truck started to burn, we quickly unbuckled our safety harnesses, fell to the roof, and crawled out the windows.

We moved a few feet away from the truck and immediately started yelling at each other again, with fists clenched and arms raised. (We were about to have a Level 1 disagreement.) However, just as we were about to really get into it, another race truck approached. They asked if we needed any help. My immediate response was a loud and definite, "No! I can handle him by myself!"

Keep in mind that with the help of the drivers in the passing truck, we might have been able to get our truck turned over and back to racing and realizing our dream. However, we were too busy trying to decide who was to blame for the crash. We had totally forgotten our commitment to our teammates, to our dream, and the months of work, planning, and development that went into making this adventure possible. How could that have happened? How could we be about to fight one another? Possibly because neither of us wanted to be the cause of our team failing to realize our dream. Neither of us wanted to be blamed for causing our truck to crash.

Tom, ever sensible, suggested that the driver in the other truck was not offering me help with our fight, he was offering us help to get the truck back on its wheels. Tom had enough sense to accept their assistance, so I reluctantly dropped my fists, and together, with the help of a tow strap and a lot of grunting, we got our truck right side up. After a brief inspection of the truck, we found that there was very little damage. With this realization, we decided to drive on and try to finish the race. Tom got back to his map-reading responsibilities, I refocused on my driving, and we were once again racing.

Approximately twenty-three hours after we left Ensenada, we crossed the finish line. We were all safe, we had fun, and we had finished. Fantastico! We had our win! Even Better, we had taken third place! Third place in the Baja 1000. We had exceeded our dreams. Wow! Let the celebration begin!

After the celebration was over and we returned to Oregon, I began to relive the entire adventure, beginning with my dream and followed by Tom and the other people forming our team. I thought about all of the time we had spent together practicing, sharing, and eventually becoming good friends. I also thought about the day of the race: the excitement of the start, the fatigue that we all felt, and then the wonderful finish.

I have relived that adventure many times. And yes, I have often thought about being upside down (literally and figuratively) in our race truck. I have also thought about what would have happened if we had continued our argument about who was the blame for causing the truck to crash. It may have ended with a fight between Tom and me, ending a good friendship, or we may have just given up our dream of finishing the race, letting down our teammates and our families. We were very close to destroying our dream, we were very close to destroying our team, we were very close to failing.

Let's take a few minutes and review the entire story from the beginning: (1) I had a dream to race Baja. (2) I shared this dream with others. (3) Five other people agreed to be a part of this dream and form a team. (4) We all made the commitments that it took to make our dreams a reality.

Now look at the crash and the upside-down truck. There we were, in the middle of the Baja desert, hanging upside down. At that point, did it make any difference that Tom didn't warn me about the rock, or that I had hit the rock and flipped the truck? Why it happened, or who was to blame, would not change where we were: we were still upside down! All the yelling, analyzing, judging, and blaming did not change the situation. Within a split second after we were upside down, Tom and I began yelling at each other. Within moments, we had forgotten our dream; we had forgotten all of our commitments, our sacrifices, and the long hours of work that we had spent in preparation for this race. We had even forgotten our friends and team members who were waiting for us at the next pit stop, counting on us to perform our roles as members of the team. We had forgotten our families and friends back home, who were supporting our efforts to realize our dream. We were so intent on blaming each other that when help did arrive in the form of other racers, we almost turned them away. In fact, for a few seconds, before we crawled out of the truck, we had even forgotten the strongest of all human instincts: survival!

Are the side effects of assigning blame becoming apparent? Are you able to recognize that as a human being, "being right" can become even more important than your dreams, than your agreements and your commitments? Maybe even more important than your own life? *Keep your listening open!* Think about this whole story. Do you know anyone who reacts in a similar way when trouble comes? Can you relate to this yourself?

The reason I shared this story with you is to point out that teams can go from winning to losing in a matter of minutes, and in the case of the Baja race story, in seconds. What happened? We turned our focus away from our dream, got upset, and focused on trying to blame each other for the accident.

We can only effectively focus on one thing in a given instant, and the one thing that we were focusing on was who to blame for hitting the rock. Our focus on blame completely distracted us from our real goals: to be safe, have fun, and finish the race. Fortunately, we were able to regain our purpose and once again refocus on our dream.

We believed that we had done everything necessary to create a winning team. We had a common, agreed-upon dream; we had open, effective communication; we were all committed and capable of completing our respective roles and responsibilities. We had done everything, except we had not prepared ourselves for resolving a destructive conflict. One of the fastest ways to destroy a team is to not be prepared to resolve destructive conflicts when they occur.

Ask!

How can we fix it?

Understanding Destructive Conflict

All teams, at one time or another, experience conflict, which generally stems from some type of disagreement. Conflict, when left unattended or unresolved, can escalate from disagreement, to anger, to blame, to resentment, to fighting, and even to war.

At one time in my life, I would have thought that the ideal situation would be to simply not have conflict. Just don't let conflict happen; don't allow it. Have you ever been on a team where there was no conflict? Where there were no disagreements? Neither have I. It is extremely rare for a family, a business, or an athletic or government team to not have some level of conflict and disagreement. Conflict is natural; however, when it escalates to a destructive level, it must be resolved or it will destroy even the strongest teams. The good news is that conflict and disagreements, when resolved, can lead to the development of an even stronger team.

In our Baja racing adventure, when we found ourselves in the middle of destructive blame and conflict, we were lucky that another racer came along to distract our attention away from our blaming and back to our dream and goals. Many teams do not have the good luck that we had; they eventually fail because of their inability to resolve their destructive conflict. Successful leaders do not depend on luck or good fortune to resolve destructive conflict. They anticipate it and prepare for it before it happens. Before we talk more about how to resolve destructive conflict, let's look at what causes it. In our Baja adventure, when we were upside down in the truck, we were disappointed, we were angry, and we were upset, and the reason was obvious. However, many times we don't really know why we are angry or upset.

Why do people get upset? What do we really know about what causes these feelings? Good questions.

Upsets

Upsets are the feelings that we have when we are unhappy or angry. Eventually, upsets will happen within all individuals and within all teams. Upsets can lead to anger, fear, blame, resentment, moodiness, depression, low productivity, lack of self-esteem, lack of confidence, and sometimes lack of control. These are only a few examples of what happens to people when they are upset. Upsets are not pleasant to experience by the people who are upset or the people around them. Have you ever been upset over anything in your life? Of course you have. We all have; it is part of being human (another sameness). We all get upset, and there appears to be an infinite number of good reasons why. However, I believe that there are only three basic reasons why we get upset. Keep your listening open.

I want to share with you an insight that I have gained over the years in dealing with my own upsets. Understanding my upsets and their causes has made my life's journey much less stressful. This awareness is also another effective leadership tool that I use to understand and relate to others who are angry and upset.

Three Causes for All Upsets

1. Unfulfilled expectations. When I expect something to happen and it doesn't (or it doesn't happen the way I expect it to happen), I get upset.

What I have discovered about myself is that many times, I create the situations that cause me to get upset. I do this by creating expectations that are unreasonable; sometimes, I have expectations of others that they do not even know about.

Many times I have expected people to call me, to help me, to take me somewhere, or to do something that they just didn't do, and I got upset. Has this ever happened to you?

I have learned that when this happens to me, before I get upset, I ask myself:

- Did they know what I expected them to do?
- Did they understand what I expected them to do?
- Were my expectations reasonable?
- Did they agree to do what I expected them to do?

I have also learned to ask myself:

- Do I expect each day of my life to be perfect, happy, harmonious, cheerful, and peaceful? Am I upset if it is not that way?
- Is it possible that I have unrealistic expectations?
- Have I ever considered that what I expect is impossible, improbable, or unlikely?

Living in another country with different customs, different expectations, and a different language has really helped me to understand some of my upsets. I am often upset because of unfulfilled expectations with people who probably have no idea of my expectations or why I am upset. Living in Mexico has helped me realize that my expectations are based on my own beliefs, my past, my customs, and my values. I have had to readjust my expectations to avoid being constantly upset. How about you? Can you eliminate some of your upsets by reevaluating your expectations or by telling others what you expect from them?

2. Thwarted intentions. When I intend to do something and something stops me from doing it, I get upset.

How many times have you intended to do something and you didn't do it? Were you upset? Were your intentions reasonable? Did you have the ability, the training, the support, the knowledge, and the time to do what you intended to do?

For example, say that I want to fly. My intention is to fly, without a plane, without a glider, without a balloon. Just me. I want to fly. What do you think my chances are of being upset? Many of us live our lives constantly upset but refuse to acknowledge our unrealistic intentions. Are your intentions setting you up for failure?

3. Unspoken communication. When there is something that I want to say and I don't say it, I get upset.

This is a big one for me. I don't like to confront people in a way that may hurt their feelings. I don't want to hurt anyone. I don't even like to tell others what I am feeling: that I am feeling hurt, or that I don't agree with the way they are doing things, or that I don't like how they are treating me. I just don't want to cause trouble. So I frequently don't say anything.

Can you relate to any of these things? Unfortunately, when I don't speak my thoughts and feelings, I continue to think about these unspoken thoughts over and over again in my head; you guessed it, this really upsets me. Ironically, sometimes I don't even know why I am upset. But through the years, I have come to recognize that many of my upsets are caused by what I didn't say.

Think of all the occasions when circumstances or people have upset you. Try to plug those upsets into one of these three categories (some upsets fit into more than one category).

Use these tools to analyze your upsets. Also use them to determine what may be causing other people to be upset by asking yourself:

1. What have they expected that they have not received?
2. What have they intended to do that they have been unable to do?
3. What is it that they would like to say that is not being said?

Coaching Hint

When you understand the real cause of an upset—yours or theirs—you can begin to focus on how to resolve those feelings and return to focusing on your desired results. Your ability to resolve upsets, within yourself and within your team, is a very important part of success. Don't live your life constantly upset!

Once you have identified the reasons for your upsets (or those of your team members), the next step is to resolve them. I have found four action steps that minimize or eliminate blame and destructive conflict within myself and my teams.

Formula for Resolving Destructive Conflict

Action Step #1
Acknowledge that there is a disagreement and/or conflict.
As simple as this step appears, there are many leaders and team members who will not even admit that there is conflict. Without successful completion of this step, you cannot begin to resolve the problem.

Action Step #2
Recognize the conflict as a team problem.
When any member of a team is involved in conflict or focuses on blaming themselves or others, and it affects their performance or the performance of the team, it is a team problem.

Action Step #3
Stop placing blame on anyone or anything.
Blame is usually a product of disagreements and conflict. Remember, once the truck is upside down, it doesn't make any difference who caused the accident. Regardless of the cause, regardless who is to blame, you are still upside down. Let go of blame; placing blame doesn't solve the problem.

Action Step #4
Turn the focus back to the desired results.
Talk about the reason the team originally came together, that dream; talk about the benefits for the team and each team member when the goal is achieved.

An effective way to introduce this method of conflict resolution to your teams is to begin by telling them the Baja story. Everyone will immediately understand how useless the yelling, arguing, and blaming was for Tom and me. This story is not threatening to anyone on your team; it doesn't affect them personally, and yet each person will relate this story to one of their own real-life conflicts. Next, introduce the four steps, explain the why for each step, answer any questions, and ask them to agree to try it for at least one month. When the time period is completed, have another meeting to evaluate the results and make any necessary changes to make it even more effective for you and your team. Try this conflict resolution process first with a few small disagreements, using them as practice runs, and then move on to larger problems as the team becomes more practiced.

I have worked with many teams that have adopted the "Upside Down Truck" symbol as a reminder that blame is a waste of time and becomes very destructive if it is not eliminated. They print copies of the picture found in Appendix A and post them throughout their living or work areas. When blame enters a conversation, everyone is invited to point to the upside-down truck as a reminder to focus on how to fix the problem and stop blaming anyone or anything.

This method of conflict resolution must be introduced *before* conflict starts. Once you are in the middle of a destructive conflict, no one will be open to listen or be coached. If you are already experiencing destructive conflict in any of your teams now, wait for the next regular team meeting and introduce the upside-down truck story and the conflict resolution steps as a new idea for the team to consider; do not introduce it as a remedy to solve the existing problem. Do not refer to previous conflicts; this will cause people to relive those painful moments and once again create the upsets that divide and destroy teams.

Coaching Hint

Team leaders must also agree to follow the four steps, especially step 3; blame must be eliminated by everyone.

With these new tools to reduce or eliminate communication problems, upsets, blame, and destructive conflict, you are ready to read the next chapter. As you read "Now Who Do We Blame?" think about how you would solve the "blame problems" if you were the coach.

Also think about what you can use from the story that will help your teams to become Even Better.

Chapter 7
Now Who Do We Blame?

A number of years ago, the University of Oregon was enjoying an outstanding beginning to its football season, winning their first four games. Much of the success was attributed to their outstanding quarterback, who I will call Bill.

One of Bill's many strengths was that he threw very few interceptions. In their fifth game, Oregon's next big challenge was to play the University of Arizona in Tucson, a team that Oregon was favored to beat. During the course of the game, Bill uncharacteristically threw four interceptions and Oregon eventually lost a close game, 22 to 17. With a cursory analysis of the preceding games—in which Bill had not thrown a single interception—logic would dictate that the cause of Oregon's loss to Arizona was Bill's four interceptions. It would have been easy for everyone to blame Bill for the loss.

Let me ask you this: Would you like to be blamed for losing a football game? Would you like to be blamed for causing your team to fail and ending an undefeated season? Of course not! Nobody wants to be blamed (this is another sameness of all human beings). Do you really believe that Bill wanted to throw those interceptions? Do you believe that he was just careless or didn't care? No? Neither do I.

Let's take a close look at the week after the loss to Arizona.

Traditionally, coaches study films of a game to analyze the good plays and the bad ones. Some coaches use the film to point out the cause of problems and to determine the cause of the mistakes (to place the blame); they show the film to the whole team repeatedly, pointing out the errors. The thinking behind these actions is, if the person who made the mistake can see and acknowledge it, and is sufficiently upset or embarrassed, they won't do it again. (This has been, and continues to be, a part of the thinking of many coaches, business and government leaders, and parents. Find out who is at fault, punish them, embarrass them, or in some way make them feel guilty, so they won't do it again.)

How would you feel if you had thrown four interceptions, your team lost the game, and you had to relive those interceptions over and over again on film with your teammates and your coaches during practice? I know that I would feel terrible, and I certainly would not look forward to Monday's practice. I would probably spend the rest of the weekend after the game worrying about the Monday film session. Fortunately, the dreaded film session did not happen. Bill was not blamed for the loss by his coaches, his teammates, or himself.

But what might have happened if he had been blamed for the loss? This is a "what if" story. I ask you to look closely to see if it sounds like what has happened on some of your own teams. The game is over. The final score: Arizona 22, Oregon 17. Bill had thrown four interceptions. Now, let's follow the story as if Bill were blamed for the loss. Bill spends the rest of the weekend brooding, feeling terrible about causing the loss. He even questions if he is good enough to play college football; his confidence level drops extremely low. He may even question his value to anyone for anything. He is dreading the Monday afternoon film session, which will undoubtedly show his four interceptions repeatedly for everyone to see. He doesn't even want to go to practice Monday. However, he reluctantly shows up with his head down. Nobody knows what to say to him, and everyone is feeling down, waiting for the review of the game film and the ax to fall.

Practice begins, and the film session starts with an analysis of the first interception. Bill notices that his throw was right on target, literally hitting his receiver in the chest. The receiver muffed the catch and knocked the ball up in the air, where a defender was waiting to make the interception. Bill squirms in his seat and feels a little better. In his mind, he is also beginning to analyze the situation: "I threw the ball well; the receiver juggled my pass! He is to blame! Not me!"

They continue to watch the film, showing the next interception; with close analysis, the team could see that Bill had thrown the ball to the correct area of the field, but the receiver had failed to get to his assigned position. There was, however, a member of the other team who got there and caught the ball: interception two. Bill feels Even Better now, knowing he had not been the cause for the first two interceptions; it was the receivers' fault. Everyone else watching knows it too. There are a couple of receivers beginning to squirm in their seats, and their position coaches are beginning to get a little edgy too.

Now, the quarterback coach is beginning to sit up a little straighter and is analyzing the receivers and their moves. Are you starting to get the picture? Now a number of people are squirming, not just Bill and the quarterback coach. As the film of the third interception begins to roll, the players can see the football bounce off the fingertips of the receiver, causing the third interception. Although it's difficult to tell if the ball was thrown incorrectly or if the receiver simply didn't catch it, Bill and his position coach notice that the linemen had failed to block correctly, which caused Bill to rush his pass. As Bill begins to feel better, the receivers feel worse, and the linemen and their coaches are starting to get a little worried.

The fourth interception was a pass that was thrown well and almost caught, but the receiver was just slightly out of position. Now Bill is feeling really good; he no longer believes that the team lost because of him, and the head coach agrees. They replay the film and start to analyze it again; this time the room is ready to blame the receivers for the loss. Under pressure, the receivers point out that they were not able to catch Bill's passes because the linemen had not been blocking correctly. With that new perspective, the team prepare to analyze the film again for the third hour to determine if the line was the reason the team lost. This time, many team members and their coaches begin to blame each other (some even blame the coach's original game plan!) for the loss.

After four hours, the film and the game had been thoroughly analyzed, and the blame had gone from Bill, to the receivers, to the linemen, to the coaches, to the defensive team, to the kicker, to the condition of the playing field, and finally to the officials. Despite all of the analyzing and finger pointing, the score at the end of the four-hour meeting was still Arizona 22, Oregon 17. Nothing had changed, except that team members were feeling increasingly ostracized and the team was on its way to a Level 1 disagreement. What happened in our what-if story was that everyone was upset and focusing on finding someone or something to blame for the loss.

Is this a situation that you have seen before? Does it appear in your business? In your family? In your cities? In your state government? In our federal government? (Try listening to the politicians in the next presidential race; you will hear all types of blame.)

Successful leaders, coaches, and parents do not spend very much time analyzing the cause of a problem. They immediately refocus on the dream, remind themselves and their fellow team members of their common goals, and start working together to move toward those mutual goals. They focus on how they can fix the problem.

We can learn a valuable lesson from this football example and from sports in general. With another game to play the next week and only limited time to prepare, there is simply not enough time to do anything but focus on the next team. In Oregon's case, they were slated the following week to play BYU, which happened to be ranked fourth in the country and had a great passing game. The coaches chose to help the players focus forward to the next game and not look back. Why? Simple. You can't change what has already happened. It's history. If you dwell on it, you are only hurting yourself more. You are once again focusing on what you don't want, and the score from that game will always be Arizona 22, Oregon 17.

In our what-if story, after the four-hour Monday horror "blame show," the players and coaches could have spent the entire week blaming each other and focusing on their mistakes. In reality, the coaches and the players all turned their focus to getting ready for their next challenge: BYU. They let the Arizona game go. It was over. Bill practiced throwing the ball accurately. The receivers practiced running the prescribed routes and catching the ball. The linemen practiced the designed blocking drills. The coaches concentrated on developing a strong game plan. The kickers practiced their kicking and focused on correct technique. The defense practiced together, focusing on the best ways to overcome BYU's strong passing game. The entire week was spent focusing on what was correct, not on what was incorrect. Oregon played BYU in a great game and won, 34–16!

In each player's heart is a dream and a hurt. When I concentrate on the injury, a synergy takes place and the hurt grows. Pretty soon, the player can think of nothing else and drops out. When I think and speak of the positive dreams, a different synergy takes place. It blazes; it sparkles. Soon the hurt is forgotten and the lifeforce of the player is called up. Therefore I only talk of dreams.
—*Vince Lombardi*

When you have players, employees, and even children, constantly focusing on not making mistakes, or on the mistakes that they have already made, a number of undesired results may occur: some will simply quit trying, some will cover up their mistakes so no one knows about them, some will get so concerned about making mistakes that they can't do anything very well, some will even get hurt or create illnesses to avoid having to participate, some will constantly look for excuses to avoid blame and look to place the blame on others, and some will simply quit the team. If there is a single, most important characteristic of a strong leader, it's the ability to keep the team focused on the dream and the desired results.

Focus

What you choose to focus on will determine how you live your life. Keep your listening open.

If you focus on being upset, you will be upset.

If you focus on blame, you will find reasons to blame yourself and those around you.

If you focus on a person's flaws, the flaws will seem to grow.

If you focus on your sadness, you will become sadder.

If you focus on pain in your body, the pain will seem to increase.

If you focus on being successful, you will find ways to succeed.

If you focus on failure, you will find ways to create failure.

If you focus on your fears, you will become afraid.

If you focus on your problems, they will seem to grow.

These are only a few examples. I encourage you to look for others. What are your experiences with your own focus? Think about a few of the things that you constantly focus on; are they things that you want to have happen, or are they things that you fear or don't want to have happen?

I was able to (rather painfully) learn about my own focus years ago when I was racing motorcycles in the Oregon desert. I was a novice rider at that time, and my learning curve was slow and frequently painful. In one race, while riding out of a wooded area onto a flat open stretch of desert, I spotted a rock about a city block away. My first thought was *Don't hit the rock*. The closer I got to the rock, the more I thought about not hitting it, so I began to issue orders in my brain for my arms to move and steer the bike safely around the rock. As I approached the rock, it became harder and harder to not focus on it; it seemed to grow and grow in my vision until, you guessed it, I hit the rock and crashed.

I had focused on the rock; ironically, by doing so I had practically ensured myself that I would hit it. As I picked myself up, I noticed that there were three or four feet on either side of the rock where I could have safely passed, had I just focused on where I wanted to go, rather than focusing on where I didn't want to go. That day, I vowed to focus on where I wanted to go instead of where I didn't want to go. With practice, I found that I could travel through very narrow openings among trees in the woods at high speeds, as long as I looked at the openings between the branches rather than the branches themselves. Later, I learned to integrate the "focus lesson" into other aspects of my life, a lesson that I continually revisit to remind myself to focus only on those things that I want for myself and for my teams.

What about you? Will you have to endure a painful experience before you learn to focus on what you want rather than on what you don't want?

We have talked about five very common team problems:

- Ineffective communication
- Destructive conflict
- Upsets
- Blame
- Loss of focus

These five problems are relatively easy to identify. However, there are many more problems that teams experience that are much more difficult to identify or to understand.

Identifying and Diagnosing Problems

All successful leaders find effective ways to identify and diagnose their team's problems.

Doctors and auto mechanics are familiar examples; they identify their customers' problems and diagnose their patients with checklists.

A doctor's checklist might include taking a patient's blood pressure, heart rate, and body temperature. They also ask their patients a series of questions and administer physical examinations to learn more about their problems. There are also numerous electronic diagnostic tools, X-ray machines, and laboratory tests—all designed to help doctors identify, diagnose, and solve the patient's problem.

Auto mechanics have checklists as well, designed to identify the customer's problem. Their checklist includes asking the car owner what the symptoms are, conducting a visual inspection of the car, checking for leaks, and looking for signs of excessive wear. Like the doctor, mechanics have a large number of diagnostic tools to help them to identify a problem and provide the necessary information to make good decisions that will solve it.

There is an important lesson to be learned from doctors and mechanics: they do not go into their offices and just think about the problem, they go to the source of the problem. They go through their checklist with the patient or with the car. Whether we are parents, politicians, business leaders, or coaches, we cannot short-circuit the diagnostic process and expect to come up with the best solution to solve the problem. During my years as a leadership and team building consultant, I developed a checklist to help me and other team leaders identify and diagnose team problems. The checklist was designed to answer questions related to each of the nine principles. This checklist is designed to work with all types of teams: families, businesses, government groups, and sports teams. I invite you to use it as it is presented, or use it as a guideline to help you develop your own checklist specific to your team and its needs.

Coaching Hint

Effective leaders don't always have the answers necessary to solve their team's problems, but they do have the questions to help them find their answers.

Team Checklist

Identify and diagnose the health of your teams. The following questions address each of the Nine Principles of Winning Teams found in Part 3. (Think of each principle as a different part of your car that the mechanic checks or a different area of your body that the doctor examines.)

Follow these guidelines:

Step 1. Select one of your teams.

Step 2. Read all of the questions.

Step 3. Add or refine questions to fit your team as necessary.

I encourage you to change, eliminate, or add to these questions and create your own personalized checklist of diagnostic tools. Every team has their own unique problems; the more specific you are when creating your questions, the more valuable the information becomes to you.

Step 4. Return to the beginning and answer all of the questions for yourself.

Keeping Score

Read each statement and circle the number that best describes what you think.

If you strongly agree with the statement, circle a 9 or 10.

If you agree but think it could be Even Better, circle a 7 or 8.

If you think maybe, but it's vague and you are unsure, circle a 5 or 6.

If you disagree or just don't know, circle a 3 or 4.
If you have never heard anything about it, circle a 1 or 2.

Principle #1: Double Win

The Double Win is the foundation principle for all successful teams. It is the basic belief that for a team to win, team leaders must invest in the growth and development of each team member. Their investment is rewarded with loyalty, commitment, teamwork, and higher levels of productivity, which translate into both individual and team success.

Statement A: There is frequent, clear communication about the goals and desired results for the team.

1 2 3 4 5 6 7 8 9 10

Statement B: There is a clear and shared understanding that each team member will benefit personally by helping the team to reach its goals.

1 2 3 4 5 6 7 8 9 10

Principle #2: Adaptation

Successful teams survive and grow because they are able to transform their problems into new opportunities for growth. This requires a culture in which constructive risk taking, trust, and openness to change are valued and encouraged. Being open to change encourages innovation, creativity, and preparation for future challenges.

Statement A: Team members are open to new ideas and change.

1 2 3 4 5 6 7 8 9 10

Statement B: Team leaders are open to new ideas and change.

1 2 3 4 5 6 7 8 9 10

Statement C: Team members are encouraged to seek and find new ways for themselves and the team to become Even Better!

1 2 3 4 5 6 7 8 9 10

Statement D: My team has an effective way (that we all understand and utilize) to resolve destructive disagreements and destructive conflict.

With team members: 1 2 3 4 5 6 7 8 9 10

With team leaders: 1 2 3 4 5 6 7 8 9 10

With other teams: 1 2 3 4 5 6 7 8 9 10

With customers: 1 2 3 4 5 6 7 8 9 10

With suppliers: 1 2 3 4 5 6 7 8 9 10

Statement E: My team has a consistent, effective way to identify and solve everyday problems.
1 2 3 4 5 6 7 8 9 10

Principle #3: Alignment

Successful teams achieve their goals and accomplish their desired results when the values, mission, and actions of all team members are in alignment. When all the members of a team are in alignment, a clear game plan can be developed to provide the direction for winning by all team members.

Statement A: All team members and team leaders, through their words and actions, are in alignment with the team's desired results. Everyone walks the talk.

1 2 3 4 5 6 7 8 9 10

Statement B: There is a clear game plan (road map) that team members understand and can follow to reach team goals.

1 2 3 4 5 6 7 8 9 10

Statement C: Team members support the team's game plan.

1 2 3 4 5 6 7 8 9 10

Principle #4: Contribution

Successful teams are developed and maintained by understanding and embracing the basic need for all people to feel that what they do is valued. Winning teams are characterized by individuals being clear about their roles and responsibilities, allowing them to understand the necessity and value of their personal contributions.

Statement A: Team members clearly understand their roles and responsibilities.

1 2 3 4 5 6 7 8 9 10

Statement B: Team members understand and appreciate the roles and responsibilities of other team members.

1 2 3 4 5 6 7 8 9 10

Statement C: Team members feel like they are valued and that their role is essential and necessary for the team to succeed.

1 2 3 4 5 6 7 8 9 10

Principle #5: Responsible Freedom

Successful teams are developed in an environment in which responsibility and freedom are emphasized. The guidelines and boundaries for responsible behavior are clearly understood and agreed upon by every team member. Every team member also has the freedom to act in accordance with his or her own personal needs within the agreed-upon boundaries of responsibility.

Statement A: There are clear boundaries and guidelines for responsible behavior that all team members agree to follow.

1 2 3 4 5 6 7 8 9 10

Statement B: Boundaries and guidelines are applied consistently to all team members.

1 2 3 4 5 6 7 8 9 10

Statement C: There is a feeling of freedom to function within the accepted boundaries and guidelines, according to each person's personal needs and values.

1 2 3 4 5 6 7 8 9 10

Principle #6: Integrity

Successful teams are developed and maintained in an environment where everyone does what they say they will do. By demonstrating their personal integrity, effective leaders receive the highest sense of integrity, commitment, and loyalty in return.

Statement A: Team members demonstrate their integrity by doing what they say they will do, when they say they will do it, and how they say they will do it.

1 2 3 4 5 6 7 8 9 10

Statement B: Team leaders demonstrate their integrity by doing what they say they will do, when and how they say they will do it.

1 2 3 4 5 6 7 8 9 10

Principle #7: Positive Learning Cycle

Effective leaders use a method of teaching in which setbacks and breakdowns are regarded as opportunities for learning rather than failures.

Statement A: Team leaders view mistakes and setbacks as opportunities to learn and grow.

1 2 3 4 5 6 7 8 9 10

Statement B: The primary competition that is encouraged within the team is to exceed previous performances, for the team and for each team member.

1 2 3 4 5 6 7 8 9 10

Principle #8: Balance of Extremes

Effective leaders are both highly directive and highly supportive in their relationships with their team members and understand the appropriate time for each style. They are able to develop a supportive environment for constructive risk taking and growth, yet instill a demand for perfection that is unyielding.

Statement A: Team leaders provide training and direction for new team members and team members with new positions, until they can effectively perform their responsibilities.

1 2 3 4 5 6 7 8 9 10

Statement B: Team leaders become less directive and more supportive of team members after they have demonstrated their understanding and mastery of their responsibilities.

1 2 3 4 5 6 7 8 9 10

Principle #9: Progressive Mastery

Effective leaders teach for steady improvement. Their method is to build one small success after another in a progressive manner, constantly reaching for a higher level of mastery. The continuous challenge for all leaders and all team members is to become Even Better! One step at a time.

Statement A: Team leaders provide training, direction, and time for team members to understand and master their responsibilities before they require them to move to a higher level of expectations and productivity.

1 2 3 4 5 6 7 8 9 10

Statement B: Team leaders recognize and understand that mistakes and errors made by team members may be the result of them functioning beyond their level of mastery.

1 2 3 4 5 6 7 8 9 10

Statement C: Some team members are working beyond their level of training, understanding, and skills.

1 2 3 4 5 6 7 8 9 10

Statement D: My team has an objective and accurate way to measure the results of the work performed:

By each team member: 1 2 3 4 5 6 7 8 9 10

By the combined team: 1 2 3 4 5 6 7 8 9 10

You have successfully completed the first step of the diagnostic process by answering these questions. Now it is time to have your team members answer these same questions.

(For best results, make copies of the checklist with the scoring table so that each team member can complete it in privacy, and set a deadline for completion.)

Ask each of your team members to answer the same questions using the same scoring scale. (Remember, your team can include all those who impact your team or who are impacted by your team.) The more people you ask, the more information you will have to make your decisions.

Start by providing all team members with the following information:

1. Mention that the primary goal of these questions is to learn what we can do together to become an Even Better team.

2. Let them know that this questionnaire is designed to help identify and solve problems. It is not a test; there are no wrong and no right answers.

3. Tell them what you are going to do with the results of the questionnaire.

4. Tell them if you intend to share the results. (If you are going to share these results, tell them how it will be shared, who it will be shared with, and the date that you will share it.)

5. I suggest that you do not have team members identify themselves on the questionnaire; ultimately, it is the responses that are important, not who made them. This lack of identification may also encourage more candid answers and reduce or eliminate team members' fear of reprimand.

(If you are using this diagnostic tool with a business or government team and there are many different subteams answering the questionnaire, ask each team member to identify the name of their subteam. This will allow you to discover any notable differences that may exist between your internal teams. Examples of subteams in business: production, sales, purchasing, shipping, administration.)

How to Interpret Your Results

After you and the members of your team have completed the questionnaire, compare your answers to theirs. You may choose to average their responses to each question; however, it is also helpful to read each questionnaire and look for responses that are considerably different from yours or from other team members. When team responses are only averaged, you may lose the extreme ends that can provide additional valuable information.

If you find that your scores for one or more of the principles are very different from the scores of your team members, you have located a problem. For example, if your answers for one of the principles are in the 8–10 range but your team's answers are in the 1–3 range, it is clear that their perception of the use of that principle is different from yours. When leaders and team members do not share the same perception of the use of a principle, it can cause a problem.

These diagnostic questions will help you find the problem areas within your teams. Create a list of the nine principles, listing them in order from the greatest disagreement to the least disagreement. Start with the principle in which there is the greatest difference between your score and the scores given by other team members, and address those principles first. There may be some principles where the team's perception is the same as yours. If the common perception is that the team is effectively implementing a principle, celebrate and move to the next principle. However, if both you and your team have a common perception that the principle is not being utilized effectively, it is obvious to everyone that work needs to be done by you as the leader as well as by your team members. The purpose of this team checklist is to identify and diagnose any problems that may exist on your team and identify the principles that need the most work. The ultimate goal of every team leader is to have all nine principles effectively implemented. Teams, the human body, and cars have one thing in common: if even a single area is not working well, it affects the ability of the whole to function correctly.

Team leaders, just like doctors and mechanics, differ in the administration and use of their checklists and the use of the information gained from them. This checklist is intended to be a model for you to use to create your own checklist. Try it; if it works, great. If you don't get the desired results, change it, make it Even Better for you and your team, and try again.

When to Solve a Problem

After you have identified and diagnosed your team's problems, it is time to decide when and how to solve them.

Leaders are challenged with yet another question in their efforts to solve their team's problems: when is the right time to start working on a problem? Our interviews with highly successful coaches, business leaders, and parents did not give us an absolute answer for this question. Many successful leaders took an aggressive approach ("Let's get started now!"), while others took a less aggressive approach ("Let's wait and see what happens before we take any action.")

I became aware of one extreme example of "wait and see" while interviewing a midlevel manager from a large manufacturing company located in the Midwest. She told me that her boss's leadership style seemed to be "avoid making any decisions, now or later." His leadership style was to give almost everyone complete freedom to make his or her own decisions, without directives, without time lines, and without any form of objective measurements of the results. That was not the answer that I was looking for; from my perspective, that kind of leadership style would probably compound their problems and reduce the chances of ever achieving their team's goals. (Her evaluation of the results seemed to confirm my opinion.) I continued to search for more answers to my questions about the best time to address a problem. After many more interviews and reflection back on my years of coaching, the answer finally became very obvious to me. The following stories may help you to answer that question for yourself.

Have you ever had a car that began to run poorly, make noises, start smoking, shake, or vibrate? I have experienced a few of those problems myself. Each time that I had a car with some sort of problem, I would just try to ignore it, hoping the problem would go away. I would continue to drive the car until it wasn't willing to go any farther. Unfortunately, when it decided to stop, it was usually late at night, snowing or raining, and I was fifty miles away from anyone who could help me. When I was forced to walk or pay a sizable towing bill to get to the nearest service area, I would remember how many times I had driven right by my local mechanic and how easy it would have been to just go in and get the problem fixed. Many times when I finally did take the car to the mechanic, I was told that if I had come in sooner, there would have been less damage, and it would have been much cheaper to repair.

Now, I know that you would never do anything that dumb: play the "wait and hope it goes away" game. However, if you have ever had a similar experience, I have a question for you: did the problem ever go away by itself? Of course not; it may have gotten better for a few weeks, maybe even a few months, but eventually it got worse and had to fixed.

Keep your answer in mind as we start our next little adventure.

Our Race in Baja

I am inviting you to join me as my co-driver in the race truck for another off-road race in Baja. Are you ready to join me? Great! Before we start, let's discuss what we will do if we have a serious disagreement during the race (no more upside-down trucks). Let's agree that, should we have any serious disagreements, we will follow the four-step conflict resolution formula (the structure that was missing when Tom and I were racing together). Let's agree that if we have a problem, we will focus on how to fix it rather than trying to decide who to blame. Agreed? Great!

Now we are ready to start our race together.

Here we go! We are off to a good start, but about four hours into the race, our truck begins to shake and vibrate. We look at each other with mutual concern, and you ask, "What do we do now?"

I have no answer for you, so we continue another few miles and approach a wooded area, where the road is deeply rutted and we are now bouncing around uncomfortably. Because the road is so rough, the vibration is not as noticeable, and we hope that it has fixed itself. We keep going, hoping that everything will hold together until we get to the finish line. However, I'm beginning to have a conversation inside my head. Should we stop and look for the problem? If we stopped, could we find it? If we found the problem, could we fix it? How much time would it take to fix it? How far is our competition ahead of us? How far back are the other trucks? Where is that vibration coming from, the front or the back of the truck? Could it be the transmission? Could it be the drive shaft? Had we hit something earlier that caused the vibration? What did we hit? Was it my fault? What should I do?

I am deeply involved in this internal conversation when ... *Bam!* Suddenly we find ourselves slammed up against a big pine tree. I can't believe it! How could that tree have jumped right out in front of us? Okay, okay, you got me. So the tree didn't jump in front of us; apparently, I drove right into it. More %$#%&#.

We jump out of the truck to check for damage and discover the very worst. We have a badly damaged radiator that can't be repaired and a broken steering arm. The race is over for us; our dreams will not be realized this year. Was it a driving error? Yes, looking back at what happened, we realize that we had a problem causing the truck to vibrate, and we kept going rather than stopping to fix it. Our decision was to continue driving, and my mind was so wrapped up thinking about what was causing the vibration that I failed to do my job: drive the truck. My focus was not on driving; it was on the vibration. (Thank you! You have correctly reminded me of what I have said many times: "You get what you focus on.") As a result, we crashed into a tree, causing an even bigger problem than the vibration, with no way to fix it for this race.

You're probably wondering why I asked you to be a part of a race effort that ended in a broken truck, with both of us sitting beside it, somewhere in Baja, Mexico.

Stay with me just a little longer for the answer.

Let's go back in the race to the point where the truck first began to vibrate. Maybe this time, with our newly gained insight, we will make a different decision and have different results. This time, as the vibration starts, I look at you and ask, "Do you feel a vibration?" You respond, "Yes; what should we do?"

The answer, based on what we have learned, is obvious: "Let's stop now and see if we can fix it."

We pull safely off the race course. We pull out our racing checklist and begin to examine the truck. We check the engine, the transmission, the tires, and the drive shaft; we look for water and oil leaks, search for loose wires, and check the fluid reservoirs. Using our checklist, we soon locate the source of our problem: we somehow managed to run over about ten feet of barbed wire. It wrapped itself around the front axle and was rubbing on the front tire, causing it to rapidly lose air. The near-flat tire and the barbed wire was causing the noise and the vibration that we were experiencing. We have discovered the problem and immediately turn our focus to fixing it. (Without any conversation about how it happened; we both learned from the first Baja race and the story about the Oregon-Arizona football game. We were determined to not get upset or blame each other or anything.) You quickly get our spare tire and replace the damaged one as I cut the barbed wire away. It took us about eight minutes to use our checklist, locate the problem, and fix it. We had worked as a team, solved our problem, and were very soon back racing again, with me focusing on my job (driving), and you focusing on the map and our navigation. Most importantly, we are safe and driving toward the finish line, moving again closer to our personal win, to finish the Baja 1000.

I should note that, in addition to continuing until we broke down, as we did in the first story, or stopping and fixing the problem, there was a third option. We could have stopped the truck, gotten out, sat down by a tree with our checklist, and had a lengthy conversation. We could have even developed a plan to fix what we believed to be the problem based on our perception and our judgment. We could have decided the problem was bad spark plugs, changed them, and drove off, believing the problem was solved. Later we would discover the vibration was still there, only worse! It's important to understand that the option of diagnosing a problem without hands-on contact with the source of the problem may actually worsen matters.

Take a few minutes to review our race together. What can be learned? In terms of a twenty-hour-plus race, eight minutes is a minimal amount of time lost. Had we chosen to continue, as we did in the first story, even if I didn't hit the tree, eventually the barbed wire would have caused the tire to go flat and maybe even caused a bad accident! It is better to stop and fix a problem than to continue and have it get worse.

What else can be learned from this race experience that can be applied to all teams? The fact that you don't recognize, acknowledge, or understand the cause of a problem doesn't mean that it doesn't exist or that it won't destroy the performance and the dreams of the team. We also learned that problems rarely (if ever) fix themselves; we learned to go to the source of the problem, diagnose it with a prepared checklist, and work together as a team to fix it.

Coaching Hint

When you believe your team may have a problem, do whatever you have to do to get the problem fixed and do it as soon as possible. Don't wait! It will rarely, if ever, go away by itself.

Once a problem has been identified and diagnosed and the decision made to solve it, the next step is to effectively eliminate it. Problems are easier to eliminate if there is a recognized, understood, and agreed-upon formula that is consistently used by team leaders and all team members. There are many different ways to solve problems; however, for me, the most reliable and effective way is to follow what I call the ABCDEs of problem solving.

ABCDE Problem-Solving Formula

A Agree that there is value for the team when the problem is solved.

B Brainstorm ways to solve the problem.

C Choose the best ideas to solve the problem.

D Do it (who is going to do what and by when?).

E Evaluate the results.

This formula will work for all teams. However, effective leaders modify their methods of implementation to fit their specific team and its problem.

Are you ready to get started? Great!

Before we start, consider these suggestions:

Follow each of the ABCDE steps in sequence. When guiding your team through the five steps, finish each step, declare it finished, and then move on to the next step. Don't return to the last step. Why? Many teams overlap the steps, combine them, or even omit one or two steps. A common example is to just eliminate Step A, seeking agreement. Without this first step, some team members may not be committed to investing the time and effort necessary to solve the problem, because they do not understand the value to the team or to themselves. Another shortcut that can lead to negative results is to overlap steps B, brainstorming, and C, choosing. Brainstorming is just that, no more; it is only to gather ideas, not to discuss or evaluate them.

Step A: Agreement

I resist calling this first step the most important, because all steps are essential to effectively solve team problems. However, it is the starting point for you as the team leader, and how you handle this step may determine the outcome for all of the other steps. Start by explaining the problem to be solved. The purpose of this step is to get team members to agree to work together to solve the problem. Agreement will follow when each team member understands the value for themselves and for the team when the problem is solved.

Move on to Step B.

Step B: Brainstorm Ways to Solve the Problem

Restate the problem that you agreed to work on from Step A and ask the team for their ideas about how the problem can be solved. All answers should be short and precise, with no details about *how* to solve the problem or *why* it is the best idea. It is up to you as the team leader to help every team member feel safe during the brainstorming step by acknowledging all ideas, both good and bad, with the same reaction: "Thank you." (They are simply ideas at this point; there will be opportunities for questions and explanations in Step C.) Ask all team members to refrain from making any comments or engaging in side talk while ideas are being given. Why? Good question. It may be interpreted as rejection or criticism by the person giving the idea. (Warning: if you, as the leader, do not keep this step safe for every team member, you will soon find that there will be no more ideas coming from individuals who feel that their answers were slighted.) Write all of the ideas on large sheets of paper and post them for all to see.

Move on to Step C.

Step C: Choose the Best Ideas to Solve the Problem

Review all of the ideas given in Step B with your team and encourage questions about them. Remind everyone to focus on the best solutions and not on who suggested them. Listen to all discussion, but do not let this step become redundant or allow a strong team member to dominate the discussion. (It is also very important for you to listen rather than direct or dominate the discussion. You already know what you think; the purpose of this step is to learn what your team members think.) Have you ever heard of paralysis by analysis? Don't let this happen to your team. When the open discussion is completed, it is time to narrow the number of ideas by placing them into one of three categories:

1. Ideas that can be implemented immediately.

2. Ideas that require more planning or an increased budget for the following year.

3. All other ideas: a source of information for future planning.

It is important that all ideas are included in one of the categories, so team members believe their ideas were appreciated.

Now is the time for you as the team leader to make a decision: which idea or ideas will be chosen to solve the problem?

Making Good Decisions

I learned two completely different ways for leaders to make decisions when I was working in the dean's office at the University of Oregon (a very consensus decision-oriented environment). I learned that consensus decisions can take endless hours of talk and compromise; they frequently end without any decision being made, which results in a lot of upset people. Until a decision is made, there is no commitment, no action steps are taken, and the problem remains unsolved.

It was also in the dean's office that I learned that my more traditional command-and-control approach of leadership didn't always work either. Even though I believed that my decisions were the best for the team, sometimes team members felt that I had failed to listen to them or to consider their ideas. The results from my C&C methods were the same as the consensus process: people were upset, and neither method solved the problem. Why? Good question. There are two essential parts to solving any problem. First, there must be a good decision made about how to solve it (there was no decision made in the dean's office process); second, the good decision must be effectively implemented by team members. There was no support by team members to implement my C&C decisions because they were not included in my decision-making process.

With this realization, I began to search for a better way to make more effective decisions, to find or create some sort of merger between consensus and C&C decision making. The ABCDE problem-solving formula provided a merger of the different ways to solve problems and allowed me to make my decisions based on input gained from my team members.

When you follow steps A, B, and C, you will usually find that team members will support your decisions and work harder in Step D to implement them, because they had input in your decision-making process.

Move on to Step D.

Step D: Do it!

After telling all team members the idea or ideas that you have chosen, it is time to begin implementation. This requires clearly defined action steps for everyone involved. Together decide *who* is going to do *what* and by *when,* and post each person's role and responsibility with a timeline for completion. When the work begins, systematically ask each team member about their timelines and progress to complete their responsibilities. During these conversations, offer your support and help if they feel it is necessary.

Some problems can be ongoing and may not be solved with the first attempt, signifying that the entire ABCDE process (or a few of the steps) may have to be repeated again and again until the problem is solved.

Step E: Evaluate the Results

Why keep score or evaluate anything or anyone? Good questions. One answer is, without some sort of reported evaluation, people will not have an accurate answer to their questions about the outcome of their effort as individuals or as members of your team. Another answer: leaders gain valuable, essential information to use for making current and future decisions. Evaluation is a necessary step to complete the problem-solving process.

There are two fundamental methods to evaluate teams and individuals. Many leaders use a combination of both.

Subjective

Subjective evaluation is based on personal observation and personal judgment.

Objective

Objective evaluation is based on the measurement of the actions taken, without bias or opinion.

First, let's look at a business that evaluates performance by observation and judgment (subjective). The president of a medium-sized company was very concerned about his firm's bottom line; profits had been down for the last few months. One day, as he passed the company's coffee room, he stopped and watched his two top salespeople standing around, drinking coffee and laughing (his observation). His immediate thought was, "Don't they know we are in trouble? Why are they standing around in the coffee room having fun, when they could be out making sales?"(his evaluation). Based on his observation and evaluation, he concluded they weren't working very hard; they were wasting valuable time. He might have also decided that they were uncaring, noncommitted, not loyal, or even lazy. The president immediately walked into the coffee room and let them know he was unhappy with their behavior. He asked them why they were just standing around drinking coffee, laughing and having a good time, when the company was having financial problems. Without waiting for an answer, he began to yell at them, using many harsh and angry words. He then stormed out of the room and returned to his office.

Later that week, he learned that the two salespeople had just delivered two of the biggest sales of the year and were congratulating each other and sharing helpful hints about how they had made their sales.

The boss had made an incorrect evaluation based on his observation and evaluation. Then he compounded the problem with a verbal attack and public reprimand of his team members. Did the boss make an honest mistake? Maybe, but it was a very costly one. No one wants to be reprimanded, especially when they believe they have done a good job.

What can a team leader do to avoid that kind of mistake? Good question. Successful leaders create systems that provide the necessary information for them to make good decisions. How do they do this? Another good question. The first step: acknowledge that subjective evaluations are not always accurate. The second step: acknowledge that accurate information requires objective measurement of performances.

If you were the president of this company and made those mistakes, what would you have done? I hope that you would have gone to the sales team, acknowledged your mistake, and asked them for their help to create a new system of measurement that rewards outstanding performance and objectively measures productivity toward personal and company goals.

Now, let's take a look at an example of objective evaluation. Leaders in sports have systems to evaluate team and individual performances based on measured, objective information. Baseball is a sport where almost every move that anyone makes is measured. When the game is over, there is a final score based on measurable results, not based on which team looked the best or which team seemed to have the better players. Individual players are also evaluated based on measurable results: batting averages, errors made, runs scored, runs batted in, rather than based on attitude or desire.

Another advantage of objective scoring: everyone knows the score at the same time.

If you had the choice, how would you like to be evaluated? Which option would you choose? Subjective, based on the leader's personal observation and evaluation, or objective, based on the measurement of your performance?

All team leaders have their own unique way to solve problems based on their style of leadership and the makeup of their team. I encourage you to use the ABCDE formula, with any modifications that you feel necessary to make it work for you and your team. Don't forget the final step: Evaluation.

Why, Why, Why, Why, Why?

Do you remember the Japanese graduate student Mizo? Mizo and I spent a lot of time discussing team leadership and the various problems that all leaders face. During one of our many conversations, I asked him if he had discovered any unique or particularly effective ways to solve problems from the many different people he had worked with and studied. He shared a story about an experience he had while working in one of the world's largest optical companies. I will never forget his answer. After he replied yes, I asked him what he had learned. He answered by rapidly repeating, "Why? Why? Why? Why? Why?" He continued his story by stating that the company created a system that required every leader to ask "Why?" at least five times for every problem they encountered, be it large or small. You probably know what my next question was: Why? I just didn't understand his answer.

To help me understand, he gave me an example of how this system of solving problems had worked in the optical company. The company had developed a system of quality control for all of their products. Their goal was zero defects, to ensure that every product that left their company was perfect. Their quality control system discovered that the prescription lenses for some glasses were not being ground correctly. The quality control team had identified the problem and soon learned that the faulty glasses were all coming from a single workstation. Rather than focusing on what or who to blame, their efforts were directed toward solving the problem. This is where they began to ask their why questions.

WHY 1: Why is this workstation and this employee making these mistakes? Many team leaders would stop at this point, assuming the employee was at fault and placing blame, maybe require more training or even fire the person for incompetence. However, at this point the quality control team asked another question.

WHY 2: Why is this employee making these mistakes? As a result of this second question, they discovered that the machine that the employee was using was not functioning correctly, which caused the glasses to be imperfect. The employee was doing his job correctly, but the machine wasn't. A grinding bit was causing the problems.

WHY 3: Why wasn't the grinding bit functioning correctly? They discovered that the pulley on the arm that turned the bit was out of tolerance, causing errors in the grinding process.

WHY 4: Why was the arm out of tolerance? It was soon discovered that the motor that turned the arm that made the bit turn was worn out, and the motor was out of balance. This might seem like a good place to stop asking why and replace the motor that was the cause of the problem to begin with. But not yet! They continued.

WHY 5: Why was the motor out of tolerance? They then discovered that the maintenance program for the motor had been eliminated about three months earlier. As a result of no inspection and no maintenance, the motor had failed to function properly.

(Remember, in this system, "Why" is asked at least five times.)

WHY 6: Why had the maintenance program stopped? From *this* question, they learned that the maintenance program was stopped to save money.

WHY 7: Why wasn't there enough money to provide maintenance for one of the essential machines that made their products? They soon learned that sales were down and there had been numerous cutbacks; there would be a shortage of money until they began to sell more glasses.

WHY 8: Why had sales decreased? This time, the problem-solving group went to the sales department to ask their question: Why?

As a direct result of this question, the company's leaders created a problem-solving team to find out why sales were down. After contacting customers, suppliers, employees, and other extended team members, they learned that their competition had created a more attractive design in eyewear, and at a lower price. They also learned that the people the company was target-marketing was not the group that bought the most glasses. The team also learned that the packaging and method for distribution of their glasses was also outdated, and that the company would benefit from a new way of marketing their products.

Wow! This entire process was created because a single workstation was producing imperfect lenses.

After my friend had completed his story—and well after I had stopped counting the number of whys—I realized that this one apparently small problem, when identified, led a multimillion-dollar company to not only ask "Why?" many times, it completely reinvented itself with a new focus and a new purpose.

I asked if the company increased sales. Did the company restore their maintenance program? Was the original employee who worked on the faulty machine thanked and acknowledged for helping to identify a problem? Yes, yes, and yes! The entire company worked together to solve its problems and to restore its desired place as a world leader in eyewear. I often think of this story when I find myself asking "why" to a problem only one time. Satisfied with my one answer, I take action steps to solve the problem, usually blaming myself or another person for causing the problem. As a result of hearing this story, I have trained myself to continue to ask "Why" at least five times—until there are no more "Why" questions left to ask.

I invite you to take this tool along with the many other leadership tools found in the Nine Principles of Winning Teams and continue your journey with confidence.

Part Five:
Tools for Life

Next to my home in Mexico is my workshop, which contains many tools: tools to use in my home, tools to work on my race car, special tools for my motorcycles, tools for my boat, tools for doing irrigation work in my yard, as well as a large assortment of tools for general use. Each tool is designed for specific tasks; however, all of my tools have one thing in common: they help me to complete tasks that I couldn't do without them. I use them to repair and maintain things, I use them when I have an emergency, and sometimes just knowing that they are there when I need them gives me confidence. These tools range from hand-me-downs to tools that I recently acquired; some perform single tasks while others have the ability to perform multiple tasks. Some have gathered rust and need a little loving care. Others are used daily. As many tools as I have, I still find it necessary to occasionally buy new ones or borrow tools from my neighbors.

There are many similarities between the tools in my shop and the tools that I have shared with you in this book. The principles, the stories, and the ideas in *Even Better!* are tools offered to you as a source of information for finding, selecting, developing, and maintaining skills that you can use with all of your teams. Select one of your teams, go through the book again, and locate those tools that will help you to solve the problems that are unique to that team. After those problems are solved, select another team and repeat the process; when team problems occur, use your tools to solve them. Tools must be used to be of value, and they will not perform without direction and skilled use. You may find that the first tool you choose does not solve the problem; select another or a combination of tools and try again and again (the only way for you to fail is to quit trying). Tools are only things that can assist in our tasks; test them with your teams until you become skilled in their use. I have not loaned you these tools; you do not have to return them. They are now yours to use, to improve, to maintain, to forget, or to lose. Take them and use them to assist you in your journey through life. Build on these tools, refine them, add to them, and make them Even Better.

(Always remember, one of the most important tools that you can use is to ask another person to help you: solicit a contribution.)

Our Journey Together

We are about to end our journey together. Thank you for agreeing to let me be your coach and for keeping your listening open to the possibility that "anything is possible." Thank you for caring enough about your family, your business, your athletes, your government, your country, and your world to want to become an Even Better team member and leader.

Continue your journey, continue to search for and find all of your dreams, and continue to ask your "Why" and "How" questions.

My personal journey will include developing new ways to pursue my lifelong dream for adventure and my desire to have fun along the way. I will continue to spend much of each year in Cabo San Lucas, Baja Sur, Mexico, riding one of my motorcycles along the beautiful coastline of the Pacific Ocean or racing my off-road car in the mountains and across the Baja desert. I will also make time to clean, polish, and refine my skills to better use all of my tools: those in my shop next to my home, and those in *Even Better!*, tools that will make my life, the lives of my loved ones, and the lives of those I come in contact with Even Better.

Thank you for letting me share with you a little about my life: my failures, my heartbreaks, and my wins.

I wish you many wins.

Coach.

Invitation

I invite you to contact me directly if you have any questions or comments about *Even Better!* or just want to talk about off-road racing or the great fishing in Baja.

LIFE IS GREAT!

coach@ballester.com

Appendix A

Feel free to copy this or to make your own sign.

Ask!

How can _we_ fix it?

Appendix B

Listed below are many of the coaches who provided much of the initial information for developing the Nine Principles of Winning Teams. Among these highly successful coaches are icons from their respective sports, leaders, innovators, and even a few mavericks, each with one single thing in common: they were all winners. I invite you to read through the list of names and take some time to learn more about their coaching careers and their lives.

John Wooden: Men's Basketball, *UCLA*
Pete Newell: Men's Basketball, *UC Berkeley*
Marv Harshman: Men's Basketball, *University of Washington*
Jerry Tarkanian: Men's Basketball, *University of Nevada at Las Vegas*
Lute Olson: Men's Basketball, *University of Arizona*
Linda Sharp: Women's Basketball, *University of Southern California*
Joan Bonvicini: Women's Basketball, *Long Beach State University*
Bob Boyd: Men's Basketball, *University of Southern California*
Morgan Wooten: Men's Basketball, *Dematha High School, Baltimore, Maryland*
Bill Walsh: NFL Football, *San Francisco 49ers*
Chris Gobrecht: Women's Basketball, *University of Washington*
Elwin Heiny: Women's Basketball, *University of Oregon*
Lou Campanelli: Men's Basketball, *UC Berkeley*
Bruce O'Neal: Men's Basketball, *University of Hawaii* and *Hawaii Volcanoes (CBA)*
Jim Harrick: Men's Basketball, *UCLA*
Laurel Tindall: Women's Gymnastics, *Seattle Pacific University*
Henretta Heiny: Women's Gymnastics, *University of Oregon*
Edwin Peery: Wrestling, *United States Naval Academy*
Ron Finley: Wrestling, *University of Oregon*
Dick Mulvihill: Men's and Women's Gymnastics, *The Gymnastics Academy, Eugene, Oregon*
Peter Kormann: Men's and Women's Gymnastics, *United States Naval Academy*

Newt Loken: Men's Gymnastics, *University of Michigan*
John Draghi: Men's Gymnastics, *Long Beach City College*
Dick Harter: Men's Professional Basketball, *Charlotte Hornets*
Rod Dedeaux: Men's Baseball, *University of Southern California*
John Scolinos: Men's Baseball, *Cal Poly Pomona*
Bobo Brayton: Men's Baseball, *Washington State University*
Norv Ritchey: Men's Baseball, *University of Oregon*
Judi Garman: Women's Softball, *Cal State Fullerton*
Gene Wettstone: Men's Gymnastics, *Penn State University*
Becky Sisley: Women's Softball, *University of Oregon*
Sid Gillman: NFL Football, *San Diego Chargers*
Don James: Football, *University of Washington*
Terry Donahue: Football, *UCLA*
Jack Patera: NFL Football, *Seattle Seahawks*
Len Casanova: Football, *University of Oregon*
Ken Morrow: Football, *Age Group, Eugene, Oregon*
Bill Dellinger: Men's Track and Field, *University of Oregon*
John Chaplain: Men's Track and Field, *University of Washington*
Bob Larson: Men's Track and Field, *UCLA*
Terry Crawford: Women's Track and Field, *University of Texas*
Bev Rouse: Women's Track and Field, *University of Arkansas*
Bev Kearney: Women's Track and Field, *University of Florida*
Stan Huntsman: Men's Track and Field, *University of Texas*
Tom Heinonen: Women's Track and Field, *University of Oregon*
Loren Seagraves: Women's Track and Field, *Louisiana State University*
Ted Banks: Men's Track and Field, *University of Texas at El Paso*
Ron Alice: Men's Track and Field, *Long Beach City College*
Linda Mulvihill: Men's and Women's Gymnastics, *The Gymnastics Academy, Eugene, Oregon*
Bill Bowerman: Men's Track and Field, *University of Oregon*
Don Robinson: Men's Gymnastics, *Arizona State University*
Bill Meade: Men's Gymnastics, *Southern Illinois University*
Dick Wolfe: Men's Gymnastics, *Cal State Fullerton*
Bobby Douglas: Wrestling, *Arizona State University*
Monte Nitzkowsky: Water Polo, *Long Beach City College*

Don Van Rossen: Men's and Women's Swimming, *University of Oregon*

Virginia Van Rossen: Men's and Women's Swimming, *University of Oregon*

Dick Erikson: Men's Rowing, *University of Washington*

Bob Ernst: Women's Rowing, *University of Washington*

Jim Verdieck: Men's Tennis, *University of Redlands*

Andre Deladrie: Men's and Women's Fencing, *United States Naval Academy*

Cliff McGrath: Men's Soccer, *Seattle Pacific University*

Bartlett Giamatti: President of Yale University, Commissioner of Major League Baseball

I also thank those many business, government, and family leaders who over the years have refined and defined this model so it can be effectively used by all teams.

Printed in the United States
By Bookmasters